I ONLY ROAST
the
ONES I LOVE

I ONLY ROAST

the

ONES I LOVE

HOW TO BUST BALLS WITHOUT BURNING BRIDGES

JEFFREY ROSS

G

Gallery Books

New York   London   Toronto   Sydney

Gallery Books
A Division of Simon & Schuster, Inc.
1230 Avenue of the America
New York, NY 10020

Copyright © 2009 by Jeffrey Ross

First Gallery Books trade paperback edition September 2010

GALLERY BOOKS and colophon are trademarks of Simon & Schuster, Inc.

For information about special discounts for bulk purchases, please contact Simon & Schuster Special Sales at 1-866-506-1949 or business@simonandschuster.com.

The Simon & Schuster Speakers Bureau can bring authors to your live event. For more information or to book an event contact the Simon & Schuster Speakers Bureau at 1-866-248-3049 or visit our website at www.simonspeakers.com.

Designed by Davina Mock-Maniscalco

Manufactured in the United States of America

10   9   8   7   6   5   4   3   2   1

Library of Congress Cataloging-in-Publication Data
Ross, Jeffrey, 1965–
   I only roast the ones I love : busting balls without burning bridges /
Jeffrey Ross.—1st Simon Spotlight Entertainment hardcover ed.
      p. cm.
   1. Roasts (Public speaking)   2. American wit and humor.   I. Title.
PN4193.R63R67 2009
808.5'1—dc22   2009021130

ISBN 978-1-4391-0140-7
ISBN 978-1-4391-0279-4 (pbk)
ISBN 978-1-4391-6420-4 (ebook)

This book is dedicated to everybody
I have ever made fun of.
Thanks for being such good sports.
(Especially you, Bea Arthur!)

This book is also a love letter
to all the great Roastmasters who came before me.
I hope they are taking turns insulting me
from that big podium in the sky.

And to the Roastmasters who will come after me,
I say . . . fuck you and happy roasting.

The first human being who hurled an insult instead of a stone was the founder of civilization.

—SIGMUND FREUD

Contents

INSULTRODUCTION

$\mathcal{M}$Y NAME IS JEFFREY ROSS, but I am commonly known as the Roastmaster General. I'm not entirely sure how I got this title, but it has stuck and I am proud of it. Most stand-up comics are self-deprecating. I'm all-deprecating. Sure, I occasionally make fun of myself—but I *specialize* in making fun of others. I'm what is commonly known as an insult comic. *Diss* is my life.

I never planned on making fun of people for a living. It happened by accident. In fact, my whole life has been a series of happy and not-so-happy accidents that have transformed me into the black belt in busting balls that I am today. I am very fond of my reputation, but I must admit that it's a blessing and a curse. I may make a nice living—but every now and then somebody wants to kill me.

With this book I offer you my philosophies of roasting, which are also my principles for a better life. If you adapt these principles to your own experiences, they will surely help guide your journey through an increasingly harsh world.

WE ALL HAVE AN
INNER ROASTMASTER

*O*UR WORLD IS FULL OF Roastmasters. Some of them are well known. But most of them are completely unknown. They live amongst us. They live inside of us. They are the part of us that occasionally says out loud what most people only dare think to themselves. The part of us that isn't afraid of severe consequences. The part of us that isn't afraid to die for a laugh. The part of us willing to take a punch from Courtney Love, if necessary.

It is the Roastmaster's belief that gracing someone you admire with unfiltered honesty is the highest form of respect you can pay them—especially when it's delivered in the form of a well-crafted joke.

Of course, not everyone has the guts to channel their inner Roastmaster. In fact, most people have the good sense NOT to insult people to their faces. Instead, they talk behind people's backs after they leave. They gossip. They whisper. They say mean things. They laugh at the weaknesses of others. This is just human nature. But a Roastmaster defies human nature. A Roastmaster goes for it. A Roastmaster tells it like it is. A Roastmaster says, "Fuck 'em if they can't take a joke." A Roastmaster kills.

A ROASTMASTER MUST HAVE THICK SKIN

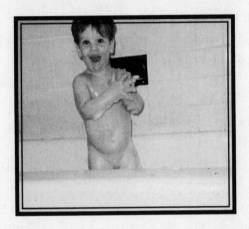

*I*F A ROASTMASTER IS GOING to dish it out, he'd better be able to take it.

I first began developing a tough exterior when I was just a baby crawling around my grandparents' cramped apartment in the Bronx. My nana Helen was making tea. While lifting the kettle from the stove to the table, she stumbled over me and spilled some boiling water onto my back. I didn't cry. No doubt I was in some kind of shock. My grandfather Pop Jack scooped me up with his giant hands and ran me fifteen blocks to the hospital. Since then, the scar behind my left shoulder serves as a reminder that my skin is thick enough to withstand anything life has to drop on it, especially insults.

I love it when other roasters take shots at me. It's a sign of love and affection. Below are some of my all-time favorites:

"Jeff Ross has a very active sex life. Every night he fucks an entire audience out of fifteen bucks apiece."

—Lisa Lampanelli

"Jeff Ross, forgive me for not recognizing you earlier— it's just that when I see a face like yours it usually has a bag of oats hanging from it."

—William Shatner

"Hey, Jeff Ross—I'm gonna give you a rap name, 'Old Ugly Bastard.' "

—Flavor Flav

"You know, Jeff does these roasts every year. It's like a holiday for him, 'Bomb Kippur.' Yeah, nigga! I know some Jew shit too!"

—Snoop Dogg

"I get a lot of flak from critics for being homophobic, but lemme tell you somethin' . . . I think having invited Jeff Ross here tonight proves how much I love the queers."

—Larry the Cable Guy

"Jeff Ross and I, we both perform for the troops. Difference is, Jeff charged for his shows."

—Toby Keith

"For your safety please avert your eyes and welcome the pork–Roastmaster General . . . Jeffrey Ross!"

—John Stamos

"What's up with Pam Anderson's implants? Pam, you've been flattened out and reinflated more times than Jeff Ross's prom date."

—Greg Geraldo

"You cannot have a roast without our next comic, but it would be great if for once we tried. He is the Michael Jordan of baseball of roasts—and is literally the only person in this room Pamela Anderson wouldn't fuck."

—Jimmy Kimmel

"Jeff Ross's dick is so small he can pee on his nuts."

—Jamie Foxx

"Jeff, we're buddies, but I've always wanted to tell you this . . . you look like they took the Friars Club and beat you in the face with it. If you looked any more like a horse, Norm Macdonald would lose ten grand on you."

—Bob Saget

"Jeff, I'd just like to thank you for doing the jokes my father used to tell me when I was seven. I'm sure this is the first time you've ever made a woman happy."

—Cloris Leachman

"Jeff Ross wants to be an old comic so bad he's having his balls lowered."

—Brian Posehn

"Jeff Ross, you're a failure and you're nothing to look at. I look at you and I remember to shave my taint . . . Jeff Ross is so ugly when he jerks off his hand throws up."

—Lisa Lampanelli

Equal opportunity ego bruising—that is the very definition of the roast. For every insult you hurl, be prepared to be insulted in kind. Your fellow roasters will be packing heat, and as my friend Snoop Dogg once told me, "Never bring a knife to a gunfight." A thick skin and a sharp wit are your best defense, so bring your A game to the podium and make every joke count.

THE ORIGINS OF THE ROAST

*H*UMAN BEINGS HAVE BEEN BUSTING one another's balls ever since we grew sacks. Early attempts at edgy humor took many forms, from the prosaic to the artistic. Evidence of prehistoric insult comedy is being unearthed as we speak. Someday soon, I hope a tape of Don Rickles roasting Frank Sinatra will surface and claim its rightful place in the Museum of Natural History—beside a North African cave drawing of a limp-wristed Homo erectus fucking a triceratops in the tuchus, where it belongs.

A growing minority of biblical scholars believe that the first use of insults in a formal dais-type setting occurred at the Last Supper. Experts believe John the Baptist stood up shortly after dessert and started making fun of Jesus's outfit.

"Hey, JC, thanks for dressing up for the occasion. Seriously, nice flip-flops. I wish I kept everything I made in summer camp."

However, it wasn't until the year 1783 that a great American patriot named Emmanuel J. Roastenberg conceived and organized the first formal insult-themed testimonial dinner.

His client and childhood friend General George Washington was about to be sworn in as the young nation's first leader, and Roastenberg thought it might be fun to honor his wooden-toothed compatriot by "dishonoring" him in front of Virginia's landed gentry.

Roastenberg decided to call the night "An Evening of Unkind Words in Tribute to Our Dear Chum," with ticket proceeds going to scurvy research. Over cigars at Washington's Mount Vernon estate, Roastenberg explained that the evening would be a ". . . fair and egalitarian exercise in wit and bawdiness." With great passion, he further reasoned that if a war hero and first president was willing to endure such a verbal lashing, it would not only add to Washington's already immense popularity but prove irrefutably to all citizens that they were finally free to criticize their leaders without fear of persecution.

"The right of the people to bear arms and hurl insults shall not be infringed. Fuck King George! Let freedom zing!" Roastenberg famously proclaimed.

Although Roastenberg was an eminent figure in colonial life, his origins are shrouded in mystery. Some historians think he was descended from a family of Prussian Jews who catered the first Thanksgiving. Another theory posits that his great-grandfather provided comedic entertainment on the *Mayflower,* and bombed so badly that he was thrown overboard. One contemporary, writing anonymously in a legal pamphlet dating from 1779, describes Roastenberg as "an irrepressibly saucy and ebullient attorney blessed by the Lorde with a sagacious wit, which has the power to illuminate truthe even as it offends gentle hearts," while another observer calls him simply "an asshole." Roastenberg was renowned for his ability to demolish friend and foe alike with a pithy, perfectly timed bon mot, which made him a formidable opponent in the courtroom. *Look at this jury. What is this, a trial by ugly?*

Some say that Roastenberg employed an indentured Irish servant to write jokes, while other accounts say he even owned a gag-writing slave. We do know for sure that invitations went out soon after General Washington agreed to participate. Roastenberg commissioned a local carpenter to build two long narrow tables, "long enough for ten men of considerable girth to sit side by side without knocking knickers." Between the two tables Roastenberg placed a preacher's pulpit borrowed from a local church, so the invited speakers would have a place to rest their notes and libations.

According to a brief report in the *Virginia Gazetteer,* the event was a rowdy and raucous affair that lasted well into the night. Legendary brewer Samuel Adams was the first to speak.

"It's no secret that leading the Revolution has given our friend George a bulgy ego. Yes, that's right, bulgy—like Ben Franklin's tits or Betsy Ross's clitoris."

"Or your liver!" yelled out John Hancock to thunderous laughter.

Betsy Ross herself leapt out of her chair to reveal a skimpy outfit she had made. "Oh, you're just jealous, Mr. Adams! If memory serves, your extremities are small and bent—like the colony of New Jersey! I do, however, apologize for my scandalous attire. I just came from the Boston T & A party! Georgie likes to salivate at the sight of my ample bosoms anyway, and I call that masturbation without representation!" America's Seamstress was a surprise hit. But it wasn't until Emmanuel J. Roastenberg himself took the pulpit that the show reached full gallop.

"Dearest Lord, I never saw so many bigwigs wearing bad wigs. I see Thomas Jefferson is here. Is this a benefit for scurvy or jungle fever? Seriously, Tom, we should party later—I hear it's singles night on the *Amistad*.

"Ben Franklin, thanks for polishing your scalp for the big show tonight. Poor guy invented electricity, bifocals, and the fire department, and he still can't get laid. He should have invented the toupee—that's about as close as he'd ever come to giving a beaver head."

"Let Freedom Zing!"

After ribbing everyone in the room, Roastenberg finally focused his attention on the guest of honor. "George's wife, Martha, wanted to be here but she's having a splinter removed from her pussy. You didn't give her crabs, you gave her termites. Folks, I've known George since he was a kid. And I think the real reason he chopped down that cherry tree was because it had more of a personality than he does!" As for Washington, the normally stoic general took the jokes in stride, claiming it was all for a good cause. Indeed, Roastenberg's "An Evening of Unkind Words in Tribute to Our Dear Chum" raised more than thirty dollars for scurvy. Despite a minor protest from the Federation of Colonial Censors (FCC), Roastenberg's bold experiment was a rousing success.

The historical significance of this night became evident a short time later during Washington's inaugural address, in which he called for a Constitutional Amendment guaranteeing free speech to all Americans. Most scholars agree that it is difficult to imagine a more influential event in our nation's history than Roastenberg's "roasting" of his dear friend and the father of our country.

MEMORABLE QUOTES FROM HISTORY'S MOST ILLUSTRIOUS ROASTS

"It's ironic the guy who discovered gravity can't get it up."

—Gottfried Leibniz at the Annual Royal Society Dinner Honoring Sir Isaac Newton, London, England, 1701

"I hear Napoleon is so short, he can go down on Josephine whilst standing up."

—British Ambassador Lord Whitworth at Le Roast du Napoléon Bonaparte, Paris, France, 1803

"I was a big fan of Herman's book *Moby-Dick*. And speaking of whales, where's Madame Melville this evening?"

—Fyodor Dostoyevsky at the New York Public Library Roast of Herman Melville, New York City, 1856

"Lou, I think maybe you'll appreciate the irony of this: I'm fucking the milkman."

—Marie Pasteur at Le Roast du Louis Pasteur, Arbois, France, 1881

"She's got one eyebrow and six boyfriends!"

—Leon Trotsky at the Roast of Frida Kahlo, Mexico City, Mexico, 1940

"Mahatma, my spiritual guide, I know you're on a hunger strike, but are you on a deodorant strike too?"

—Jawaharlal Nehru at the Roast of Mahatma Gandhi, Bombay, India, 1940

"Nice beard, Fidel. What did you do, go down on it and come up with it?"

—Che Guevara at El Roast del Fidel Castro a la Hotel Nacional, Havana, Cuba, 1959

1. Honoree
2. The Roastmaster or Roastmistress
3. The Roasters
4. The Audience
5. The Venue
6. The Dais
7. The Podium
8. The Microphon
9. Custom Artwor
10. The Booze

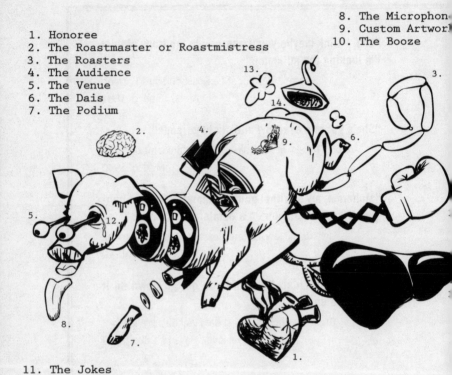

11. The Jokes
12. Dash of Sincerity
13. The Surprises
14. The Rebuttal

RECIPE FOR A ROAST

*T*AKE A WALK, BASEBALL! GO fuck your sister, NAS-CAR! Roasting is quickly becoming America's new national pastime.

Whether it's professional insultarians making fun of a celebrity or just regular folks roasting a loved one, the art of busting balls is boldly on the rise. You may have noticed that homemade roasts seem to be popping up every weekend in backyards, catering halls, dormitories, and convents all over this great land. As Americans, there is no healthier way to exercise our right to free speech than by saying atrocious things about other people in public.

However, you can't always wait for an invitation. Occasionally you may want to whip up a roast yourself. But beware—ingredients may vary and no two roasts ever turn out the same. But one thing is for sure, people will talk about it forever.

Ingredients

THE HONOREE

As you might expect, the hardest part of producing a roast is getting someone to volunteer to be *ripped a new one* in front of other people. That is why your honoree must feel protected. That's why we only roast the ones we love.

Ideally, the honoree should be an exceptional individual of high regard. You know, someone who deserves a pat on the back and a kick in the pants. I believe the best roasts occur when you laud an accomplished person on a special occasion. Perhaps they are Teacher of the Year or Employee of the Month or Fuck-face of the Century. Maybe they just got a divorce or a hysterectomy. A personal roasting can even be the perfect birthday gift for the man who has everything. That's what I gave Jimmy Kimmel for his fortieth birthday, at a party where he was surrounded by his huge and hairy extended family—most of whom are also employees on his long-running late-night TV show.

"Congratulations, Jimmy—how is it possible to give nepotism an even worse name? Seriously, I haven't seen a family bond like this since Jerry Lee Lewis fucked his cousin. And imagine how much better off your relatives would be if they were related to Jay Leno?"

When I was asked about producing a roast for boxer Mike Tyson I felt I had to decline because under my own criteria he just didn't seem a worthy recipient. I just couldn't wrap my brain around honoring a convicted rapist and part-time cannibal. I also once refused a request by the great Howard Stern to roast my fellow Jerseyite Artie Lange on the radio. When I asked their producer Gary Dell'Abate what charity they were raising money for by roasting Artie, he said there wasn't one. "We're just doing it for shits and giggles," Gary said. I responded that that wasn't a good enough reason for me to honor somebody I love as much as Artie and politely declined.

Months later, Artie mentioned on the radio that he would soon be traveling to a war zone to entertain the troops. When I heard this I called Gary back and asked if I could come give Artie a personal mini-roast in honor of his upcoming trip. He agreed, so I came into Howard's studio and let it rip: "It's no coincidence that Artie has become patriotic because his weight just hit 9/11. Artie, be careful—it's dangerous over there. What are you gonna do? Wear a bulletproof and a button-proof vest? I hear Artie's USO codename is Blob Hope."

All I'm saying is you never roast somebody *just because*. I believe it should benefit a good cause or be based around an important moment in the honoree's life, like a marriage, graduation, or retirement. I once roasted my cousin Mikey at his going-away party. After two years of living in my guesthouse, it was finally time for my comatose Cuban cousin to migrate back to his natural habitat in Miami. Don't get me wrong, I love Cousin Mikey with all my heart and half my refrigerator—but when he wasn't lounging by my pool or playing Xbox, he was sound asleep on my sofa. Now he was finally moving on with his life and what better farewell could there be than creating a special night in his honor? I also knew Cousin Mikey would be a great guy to roast because he has a huge heart and even huger ears. Plus, he had just spent two crappy weeks in the hospital because his diabetes had spiraled out of control and an evening of laughs seemed to be just what the doctor ordered.

Our pal Brendan came up with the idea for the roast. He owns a fledgling animation studio where Cousin Mikey allegedly worked, and even though Brendan considered Mikey "The PA" Gonzalez to be the least productive production assistant in television history, he still loved the guy and wanted to give him a big send-off.

Brendan decided that donations at the door would go toward gas money for Cousin Mikey's long drive back to south Florida, and he gave the whole evening a *Scarface* theme because that is Mikey's all-time favorite movie. Cousin Mikey was extremely flattered by Brendan's generous gesture. After all, who doesn't love being the center of attention—even when there's a target on your forehead? The story of roasting my cousin Mikey provides an object lesson in gathering the ingredients for a deliciously disrespectful roast.

THE ROASTMASTER OR ROASTMISTRESS

Every roast has an emcee, or *Roastmaster*. This person sets the tone for the whole evening and should have a very close connection to the guest of honor—such as being a teammate, roommate, soulmate, classmate, or cellmate.

Being asked to serve as someone's Roastmaster is considered an honor unto itself—on par with being a best man or a pallbearer or a fluffer. This is why I was so tickled to serve as Roastmaster at my cousin Mikey's farewell roast. He and I are like brothers and I wanted to do right by him.

Typically, the Roastmaster has crucial responsibilities, such as introducing the other roasters and deciding the order in which they speak. The later in the line-up somebody goes on, the harder it is to find untapped angles to joke about. On too many painful occasions, somebody has done the exact same joke as mine right before me. In this situation, I have no choice but to drop it from my script. This can be very frustrating, but it's just one of the inherent challenges of the game. People will hassle you to go on early, but remember that a Roastmaster saves his strongest acts for the end of the show. If your aunt Lulu can fart the alphabet, you may want to put her on last.

Of course, at a roast, anything can happen and a Roastmaster must stay engaged at all times. I once physically dragged Andy Dick offstage because he wouldn't stop humping Carson Daly's leg. Another time I helped lift Gene Simmons from KISS off the floor after he stumbled over his own seven-inch platform boots. And I once dragged sports anchor Dana Jacobson away from the podium because she was guzzling Grey Goose and screaming "Fuck Jesus!" to the football coach of Notre Dame. To be a great Roastmaster one must not only command respect—but *demand* it.

THE ROASTERS

A well-done roast should have no less than five speakers and no more than a dozen. The trick is to cover every angle of the guest of honor's life without getting too redundant. Aim for variety. Try tracking down an old teacher, coach, or ex-girlfriend with a great rack and a good sense of humor. Mikey's roasters were a mixed bag of friends, co-workers, and childhood homeys who flew up from Miami for the occasion.

When I produced MTV's roast for Carson Daly, the beautiful actress Jennifer Love Hewitt got some of the biggest laughs of the night when she walked out and said, "Hey, Carson—remember me? Girlfriend number 147?" Then she went on to read an old love letter from him that revealed he used to wear her nail polish. In the end, they hugged it out and it was a long-overdue reunion that Carson really enjoyed. At least until his lifelong pal Jimmy Kimmel came out and delivered what would have been the best-man speech at Carson's wedding.

I truly believe great roasts are the extension of great friendships. That is why the guest of honor must be surrounded by loved ones. Ideally, an honoree should feel like he's Frank Sinatra and his friends are the Rat Pack. If the center of attention is having a good time, then everybody else will too. The ultimate goal is to have everyone leave at the end of the night hoping they too will get roasted by their friends someday.

THE AUDIENCE

Getting a crowd for a roast is never difficult. For some reason we Americans love the sheer spectacle of public humiliation. Back in the day, entire populations would fill a town square just to watch people get tarred and feathered. It's basic human nature to derive pleasure from watching other people squirm—especially if it's for an important cause. That's why so many roasts are produced by charity organizations. I mean, who isn't willing to buy a ticket to watch somebody be called a lazy good-for-nothing schmuck in the name of pulmonary heart disease? Believe me, if you roast them, they will come.

THE VENUE

Because we were expecting a big crowd for Cousin Mikey's roast, we rented out The Comedy Store on a night they would normally be closed for fumigating. However, my experience is that you can hold a roast practically anywhere. I once roasted Johnny Knoxville in the back of a van in Burbank and Rachael Ray in a baseball stadium in Houston. I once roasted Drew Carey on a flatbed truck in Fallujah and my uncle Murray in a whorehouse in Havana. Just make sure you pick a place with plenty of parking and a back door, because occasionally a Roastmaster needs to get out of Dodge.

THE DAIS

The *dais* is the long narrow table where all the roasters and other honored guests sit in the most traditional of roast settings. If long tables are not available or do not fit in the room, a few couches or chairs assembled side by side will do just fine. Sitting on blankets is for picnics, poetry readings, and pussies—and this is a roast you're producing, for crying out loud.

As the producer it is your responsibility to make sure the dais is safe and secure. One time at the Friars Club, we were in the middle of roasting Drew Carey when suddenly ninety-three-year-old comedian Joey Adams fell off the back of the elevated dais. The poor old guy just lay squirming behind a curtain while an oblivious Kip Addotta continued his riff about having anal sex with Drew Carey in the bathroom of a turkey farm. Paramedics eventually arrived and took Joey in for tests. The audience never knew a thing. In the end, it all worked out. Joey Adams lived and Kip Addotta killed.

THE PODIUM

Ideally, the dais should be separated in the middle by a podium or lectern. This will give the roasters a place to rest their notes, drinks, and firearms.

The podium should be sturdy and relatively simple in appearance. I recently saw a roast for stoner comic movie legends Cheech and Chong on TV, where the producers tried to be cute by creating a podium that looked like a giant bong with smoke coming out of it. Halfway through the show, Penn & Teller were attempting a magic trick when Penn's hand accidentally bumped the side of the podium. The flimsy prop collapsed in a smoldering heap and couldn't be repaired or removed. Consequently, each roaster was forced to perform while holding their notes and noses in front of a smoking pile of shit, just like *Up in Smoke,* which, ironically, is also how I would have described Cheech and Chong's movie career if only they had the guts to invite me to their roast that night.

THE MICROPHONES

A firmly mounted unidirectional microphone with an adjustable gooseneck stand is an essential ingredient of any roast. As the Roastmaster General, I feel it is my duty to warn you never to skimp on the sound system. Also, you should always get a backup microphone just in case one of the roasters accidentally drops it, breaks it, or inserts it into their private parts. (That means you, Aunt Lulu!) Like I stated earlier, anything can happen. Be prepared.

CUSTOM ARTWORK

It's always a fun idea to track down an embarrassing picture of the guest of honor and affix it to the front of the podium. Photoshopping in a Hitler moustache or Frankenstein bolts is always a fun option. Because my cousin Mikey worked with animation artists, they designed invitations and a special poster for his roast that depicted him as a naked piglet with pineapple rings stuck in his butt cheeks, ready to get barbecued. Not only did this image help set the mood, but it gave the whole event a certain artistic flair.

THE BOOZE

Booze is the secret ingredient of any roast. Liberal amounts of libations will loosen everybody's lips and help the verbal abuse go down easier. Personally, I like to drink scotch on the rocks. It makes my mind soar and my balls tingle. However, you do have to be careful at these events. At the roast of Pam Anderson, I practically had to be carried out by my pals Aaron Lee and Eddy Friedfeld after Andy Dick put a roofie in my drink. I don't have any proof, but it was probably payback for saying, "Andy Dick's sole mission in life is to give AIDS back to the monkeys."

By the time I called Cousin Mikey's roast to order, most of

his friends and loved ones were on their third round of Cuban mojitos. This helped put everybody in the laughing mood as I introduced our honoree. With a drink in his hand, a grin on his face, and a silk Tony Montana–inspired shirt on his back, Cousin Mikey was escorted to his throne by our sexy twin friends Bibi and Fifi Poubelle, who enthusiastically embraced the *Scarface* theme by dressing as hookers from Havana. Everyone raised a glass as Mikey assumed the position.

THE JOKES

One should always come to a roast armed with an array of salty zingers. Showing up at a roast without jokes is like driving a car without a motor. Don't assume you can just go up and riff. Only Don Rickles can do that. You're not as talented as he is, although you're almost certainly better-looking.

As you write your jokes, don't censor yourself. Everyone in the audience wants you to hit hard, and you owe it to the guest of honor to bring the pain. However, before I roasted the scary monster Shaquille O'Neal I was terrified that he might not understand what he was in for. I'd seen his temper flare up before and I honestly thought that if I said the wrong thing he might just rip my head off and eat it on national television. When I ran into him at rehearsal, I asked as gingerly as possible if he was the type to be easily offended. He told me the only thing that I could do that would piss him off was to go soft on him. He said, "Do what you do, Ross. Nobody ever told me to hold back on the basketball court—so you shouldn't hold back on your jokes. If people think you let me off easy, only then will I look bad." The big man's encouragement gave me the go-ahead to say crazy stuff like, "Shaq, your knuckles look scraped—did you walk here? You're so big and clumsy, watching you play basketball is like watching a retard fuck. But seriously, Shaq—you were great in *The Green Mile*." My license to kill was further validated by Roastmaster Jamie Foxx, who kicked into the air yelling "Fuck yeah!" every time I landed a big joke.

Even with all my goodwill and experience, it still takes me weeks to properly prepare for a roast. I start by asking myself questions from every conceivable angle. What does everybody hate about this li'l angel? What does everybody love about this big asshole? Sometimes I even hang up pictures of the guest of honor around my house so I can become more familiar with how uniquely unattractive they are. When possible I even reach out to them personally and take them to lunch or dinner sometime before the big night. This way I can get into their heads and find out their sensitive areas. Like a shark, a Roastmaster circles his prey before going in for the kill.

Serving as Roastmaster for Cousin Mikey's farewell party meant I got first crack at him. I began with a reference to the large crowd, "Wow, Mikey—this turnout is clearly a testament of how excited we all are that you're getting the fuck out of town. . . . Oh, Mikey, what a cruel twist of fate to have such large ears but nothing in between them. Seriously, when you were a kid, did you use your ears to swim here from Cuba? In case you didn't know, my cousin Mikey is half Cuban and half Jewish. That's right, he's a Jew-ban. Everyone knows Mikey loves to play Xbox because that's the only box he can get into. Seriously, Mikey, forget animation—you should work in a masturbation studio. You think you're Tony Montana? Please. You're about as tough as Hannah Montana. Of course Mikey is obsessed with *Scarface*—which reminds me . . . Mikey, say hello to my little friend—his name is Unemployment."

When preparing a roast, I never write a specific number of jokes. I usually just keep going until I can't think of anything else mean to say. That's when I know I'm done. Also, try to keep in mind that your jokes are precious. For maximum effect, they must be kept secret until the big show.

A DASH OF SINCERITY

At the end of your speech, it's traditional to throw in something affectionate. At Cousin Mikey's roast I said, "Everybody who knows Mikey understands that he is a compassionate guy and a true sweetheart. His time in Cali was not always easy, but he surely enriched all our lives while he was here. Mikey is not only my cousin but he's one of my best friends—and I'm gonna miss him. In fact, we're all gonna miss you. I love you, Cuz."

It was a beautiful moment. Cousin Mikey teared up. I even got a little weepy. Before the entire roast melted into a sugary disaster, I banged my fist on the podium and said, "Okay, Mikey—you ready for this?" He took a swig of his drink and said, "Bring it on, Cousin Roastmaster." Then one by one I presented a ragtag roster of roasters, who all paid tribute in their own different ways and ended by saying something sweet about the honoree. Cousin Mikey loved every minute of it.

THE SURPRISES

No roast is truly complete without a couple of "holy shit" moments. Because MTV's *Jackass* is Cousin Mikey's favorite show of all time, I secretly invited one of its most popular cast members to his roast. The crazy and unpredictable Steve-O agreed to perform a physical stunt in which he would have Cousin Mikey assist him in stapling his testicles to his inner thigh.

Unfortunately and unsurprisingly, Steve-O showed up too wasted to perform the stunt. Instead he just showed off his latest conquest—a beautiful blond Norwegian supermodel—and then went on to recite an unintelligible rap song that had nothing to do with anything. Still, it was wonderful that he showed up because it allowed me to mention to the entire audience that after the roast we were all going to take turns finger-banging "Steve-O's transvestite girlfriend."

THE REBUTTAL

After enduring an evening of insults, the now disheveled guest of honor approached the podium for his customary last licks. Cousin Mikey graciously thanked me for serving as the evening's Roastmaster before zinging me. He said, "All my friends had the same response when I first told them I was moving out to California to live with my famous cousin, Jeff Ross. They said, 'Who?'"

Now that he'd gotten his first laugh, he had the confidence to go after the dais as a whole. "I was worried you guys were gonna make fun of my beloved Miami Dolphins, but then I remembered . . . queers don't watch football." Next he turned to his boss at the animation studio and said, "I'd seriously like to thank Brendan for teaching me the business—the business of drinking and smoking weed."

Cousin Mikey went on to acknowledge every person who roasted him, before wrapping it up with a short farewell: "I'll be taking a piece of everyone here back with me to Miami. All of you are great friends. Loyalty means everything to me. You guys were always there for me whenever I needed help or to be cared for. I love you guys—you won't be forgotten. Thank you."

After soaking in the standing ovation, Cousin Mikey walked around and hugged everybody in the place, including the waitresses and the bathroom attendant. The next morning he packed his *Scarface* shirts and his Xbox into his PT Cruiser and headed for home. A few days later, he called to tell me he had arrived safely and that getting his balls busted by all of his buddies was the best night of his life.

Being the honoree of a roast is the ultimate ego trip. And roasting somebody is an incredible rush. But actually *producing* an entire show to benefit a good cause and honor somebody you love is a major accomplishment. So don't forget to tape it.

A ROASTMASTER
SAVES LIVES

*P*EOPLE ALWAYS ASK ME, "WHAT'S the best part of being a Roastmaster?" I don't even have to give the question a second thought. By far the most gratifying thing about my profession is the fact that I occasionally save lives through my roasting duties. Lest you think I'm not playing with a full dais after making such a grandiose statement, allow me to explain.

You see, a true Roastmaster is an expert in the art of discovering and pointing out flaws and foibles. When these flaws and foibles include reckless, out-of-control behavior, the course of a roast victim's life can be altered and their imminent self-destruction averted. Take the case of the charming American songbird Courtney Love.

I met the demure Madame Love in the summer of 2005 at The Comedy Central Roast of Pamela Anderson. In all fairness, she was perfectly lucid and friendly when I introduced myself backstage. I've always been a big fan of her band Hole, so I sought her out before the show and said, "Courtney, I'd like to introduce myself. I'm Jeffrey Ross, I'm one of the roasters. I just want to say I'm a really big fan."

"Oh, why, thank you, Mr. Ross. Enchantée de faire votre connaissance," she answered in perfect French, while shaking my hand with the firm grip of a nonpsychotic, law-abiding woman of the world. But before our conversation could turn to politics or art, she disappeared into the bathroom with Andy Dick—which is never, I repeat, NEVER, a good thing to do. I tried to tell myself they were just going to exchange makeup tips or muffin recipes, but deep down I knew this roast was shaping up to be a crazy and possibly contagious catastrophe.

Sure enough, the second the cameras started rolling, Courtney transformed into a sloppy, repulsive mess. It was as if Joel Gallen, the director, flipped the "raging crackhead" switch. Greg Geraldo went on first and set the tone for the evening with the lead-in: "Speaking of anal warts . . . Courtney Love is here." The crowd burst into applause. Courtney stood up, gave everybody the finger, and flashed her vagina for the cameras. People tuning in late must have thought they were watching a new game show, "Who Can Be the Most Unhinged and Incoherent?"

The truth is, Courtney craved the attention. She was egging on the roasters and would occasionally raise her hand and beg to be picked on—sort of like a whacked-out Arnold Horshack. Sarah Silverman said it best, "You never know which Courtney Love is gonna show up . . . the smeared-lipstick crazy coke whore or the violent smeared-lipstick crazy coke whore." Nick Dipaolo even tried to be complimentary: "Courtney Love was amazing in the movie *The People vs. Larry Flynt*. She played a white trash psychotic stripper who was addicted to heroin. . . ." He paused as the audience clapped in appreciation of her Oscar-nominated performance. Nick continued, "What did you do to prepare for that role, follow yourself around for a year?" Courtney stood up, flashed her breasts, and yelled, "I've been sober for a year!" A leap year, maybe.

Of course, I got pretty wasted that night too. Even worse, I was sitting next to Andy Dick. Rest assured I wasn't in charge of the seating arrangements. But, hey, it's not like I tongue-kissed the guy or anything. Well, technically, our tongues did touch, but like I alluded to earlier I think it's because he slipped a lude into one of the six or eight Dewar's on the rocks I downed that night.

I still have misgivings about the lip-lock, which was kindly cut out of the show. I have no recollection of it whatsoever, but by all eyewitness accounts, sometime toward the end of the roast, Andy squished up against me and stuck his tongue all the way out and I just went for it. Obviously, I'm not at all homophobic— some of my most famous friends are secretly gay. I am, however, a germophobe. Making out with Andy Dick is roughly equivalent to canoodling with the rim of a toilet bowl. Miraculously, I survived the sedated smooch without contracting a flesh-eating disease. Call it the luck of the Roastmaster.

During a break in the action, I asked the evening's Roastmaster Jimmy Kimmel about a certain Courtney Love joke scribbled in the margin of my notes. He read it and immediately told me not to do it because it was just too harsh. But as I readied myself for my time at the podium, Miss Love's antics continued. She flailed, mumbled, and cursed. She belched, farted, babbled, and drooled. Basically she did whatever she could to upstage whoever was speaking. At one point, Kimmel attempted to physically hold her down. Again she declared, "I've been sober for a year!" Finally Jimmy said, "I hope that's not true—because if you're *not* on drugs you've got problems." I was so embarrassed for her, I almost decided to leave her out of my roast. But then it became so

clear to me—a brutally honest roasting might set this talented but troubled woman back on the right path.

And so it was with a certain gravitas and sense of purpose that I took the podium. Well, actually, I swaggered onstage in a full-length fur coat that made me look like Superfly's accountant.

Courtney threw ice at me as I taunted the animal rights activist and bombshell of the hour, Pamela Anderson. Later I told Pamela I thought it was hypocritical that she cared so much about animal rights when she had been torturing her own beaver for years. These jokes were all in good fun and dog lovers needn't worry—the coat was 30 percent puppy, tops. Pam was a great sport as I riffed on a few other topics, including her cavernous vagina. "Is it true they give free donkey rides to the bottom?" I asked as politely as possible.

When I finished teasing Pammy and zeroed in on Courtney, I knew my duties had become more serious. My goal crystallized as I watched her pick her nose and hump her armrest simultaneously. I was determined to roast this rock and roller into rehab.

I started slow: "Courtney Love, you're like the girl next door. If you happen to live next to a methadone clinic." Everybody laughed, including Courtney who stood up and motioned for me to bring it on. Since she was now asking for it in every sense of the word, I took a deep breath and went in for the kill. In a booming voice I said, "Folks, how is it possible that Courtney Love looks worse than Kurt Cobain?"

It's hard to describe the sound of a thousand jaws dropping at once—but that's all I could hear in that moment.

This is the joke most often trotted out when people are trying to prove that I am amoral, twisted, reckless, fearless, evil, and demented. In fact, the network censors nearly cut it from the show. A review in the *New York Times* quoted me and said, "Is that line even legal?"

Ironically, I believe this is the joke that saved Courtney Love's life. When they heard it, she and Pam exchanged a look of utter

disbelief. Then Courtney heaved herself out of her chair and stumbled in my direction as if she was going to pounce on me like a drug-addled mother lion protecting her cubs.

And why not? I had just taken a shot at her and the deceased father of her child. But I did it with words and that's why she ultimately sat back down and resumed staring into space, only this time with a slightly more thoughtful expression on her lipstick-smeared face. You see, a Roastmaster uses words to touch hearts and alter minds, even if sometimes we offend a few folks along the way. I knew she wasn't mad at me because only moments later she ran over to me, got down on her knees, and pretended to blow me.

The very next day, a dozen roses showed up at my apartment from Pamela Anderson, thanking me for doing the roast and supporting her charity. That same day I read in the paper that Courtney Love had entered rehab. Many people say it was my verbal beatdown that convinced her that she needed help. A short time later I read that the rehab facility was suing Courtney for unpaid bills. Okay, so maybe I didn't reform her completely. But I did do my small part to bring about some change—and a Roastmaster should always be an agent of change.

MY SECRETS FOR WRITING ROAST JOKES

THINKING UP MEAN THINGS TO say is easy, but making them funny is a mysterious craft with no set rules. I wish there were a delicious smoothie full of creative juices that I could drink every morning, but the truth is sometimes you just have to stare into space until an idea pops into your brain. I once heard the comedian Paul Reiser describe joke writing as staring at the faucet, waiting for the leak. Personally, I believe it's dangerous to examine too closely how the human nervous system creates these sparks of vitriolic insouciance. In fact, usually analyzing comedy gives me a headache, but for you people I'm willing to pop a couple of Advil and deconstruct my process.

Basically, I see funny insults as a combination of wit, timing, and animosity. Sometimes a great joke just drops from the sky and lands on my head like bird shit. Other times, I have to bang my head against the wall just to come up with an okay joke. Sometimes a shitty joke and a great joke pop into my head all at once. Then my aunt Donna calls and I forget both of them.

Here are some more of my secrets to help you get started on your joke-writing journey.

• OPENERS

Your first few jokes should try to encapsulate the event. There's no better way to win over an audience than by sizing up the entire dais in a single sentence.

> "Congratulations, Carla! Are these your bridesmaids, or the winners of an Octo-Mom look-alike contest?"

> "Hey Pete, how'd you get all these high-class folks to show up for your birthday? What, was the Waffle House closed for renovations?"

For practice, look around right now and see if you can think up a single line that epitomizes your surroundings. If the room is full of nobodies (and let's face it, it probably will be), you might say, "This isn't a who's-who—it's a who cares." At the hillbilly heavy roast for Larry the Cable Guy I said, "This is the first show I've ever been to where the stars brought their own trailers." At the nearly 100 percent chocolate roast of Emmitt Smith I said, "This isn't a roast—it's a barbecue." At the paisan-populated roast of Pat Cooper I said, "This isn't a roast—it's a grease fire." At the oddball-infested roast of Bob Saget I said, "Look around. This is what happens when you book a dais off Craigslist." Okay, enough already. You get it.

• TWOFERS

It's especially fun to nail two people with one line. "Hey, Uncle Joe, I dunno what stinks worse—your feet or Aunt Donna's cooking."

At a roast for the *Today Show*'s Matt Lauer, I devised a killer twofer around his fluffy interviewing style, "Let's face it, Matt's questions are softer than Neil Simon's cock." Trust me, insulting two birds with one stone won't diminish the impact of the joke— it only doubles the laugh. In the above case it actually tripled the laugh, because as soon as I said it, a sexy blonde in the front row leaped out of her chair and said, "Neil Simon's cock works just fine! I should know! I'm his wife!"

• CROSSBREEDERS

These are some of the most fun jokes to write. All you really have to do is stare at a picture of the person you're roasting and imagine how such a creature was created. Let your genealogical imagination run wild.

> Drew Carey: You look like Buddy Holly and Barney
> Rubble had a baby and then peed on it.

> Gene Simmons: You look like a rabbi fucked an Indian
> chief.

> Uncle Murray: You look like Great-Grandma Rosie was
> raped by an owl.

For practice, look at yourself in the mirror. That's what I do. Clearly I look like Rick Moranis and Walter Matthau had a baby and then punched it in the face.

• TAGS

A tag is a little joke that goes after a big joke. For example, if the joke is "Larry the Cable Guy has fucked so many farm animals down South they call him Larry the Stable Guy," then the tag is "Remember, Larry, neigh means neigh."

Another example: At the roast for sitcom dad turned perverted comic Bob Saget I said, "You may not know Bob used to give Mary-Kate acting lessons. He'd say, 'Shh . . . act like this never happened.' Then I dropped the tag, which was a play on the Olsen twins' catchphrase from the show, "She'd be like, 'You got it, dude!' "

By tagging your jokes you can use a single setup to get multiple laughs. This is the key to killing.

• SAVERS

One of the great challenges of performing a roast is that you are trying out material for the first time. Chances are some of these jokes will crash and burn. That's when you tell a "saver" such as, "Hey, I don't even do comedy—I'm here to put the chairs up after you people leave." Some of my most dependable savers are "Give me a break, folks, my writers are on strike." "Well, I guess it's never too late for me to apply to law school." "Good thing my dad owns this place." If I happen to make a joke about somebody who isn't there and it gets a groan, I always save it by saying, "Is he here? No? Then fuck him!"

The concept of a saver was first explained to me over chicken salad sandwiches at the Friars Club by the great Roastmaster Milton Berle, who had perhaps the most reliable one ever. When one of his roast jokes bombed he'd nonchalantly flip to his next index card and say, "Here's another one you may not care for . . ."

• KEEP YOUR DISTANCE

For harsher jokes, you may want to distance yourself slightly from the comedic accusation. The goal here is to deflect responsibility. In other words, say that you're not really saying what you're saying.

> "I'm not saying her ass is big, but when she shakes it the tides change."

> "I'm not saying her cooking is bad, but I think my vomit speaks for itself."

Creating this slight buffer zone between you and the joke will help you dish out the hard stuff without being overly offensive.

• PLAYING DUMB

The trick here is to say something horrible in the form of an innocent question.

> "Tony, clear something up for me—is that a very bad toupee or a very sick ferret?"

> "Nice blouse, Laura, where'd you get it, Forever 41?"

> "Hey, Uncle Herman—are those your teeth or did you crash your Chrysler into a piano store?"

In roasts, as in life, playing dumb will help you get away with a lot. Some of you don't even have to play.

• CLOSERS

Your "closer" should not only be your strongest joke but should also express a sentiment that sums up the overall message of your roast. Ideally it should be a backhanded compliment. At the Larry the Cable Guy roast I closed by saying, "Ladies and gentlemen, ask not what your country can Git-R-Done for you, ask how this inbred cousin fucker made twenty-eight million bucks last year."

However, the bigger the build-up your closer has, the better. At the Saget roast, I finished by paying tribute to the guest of honor's love of expletives: "Folks, you may have noticed I didn't curse at all tonight because I didn't want to compete with the master. Out of all the comics I know, you've got the filthiest mouth and the kindest heart—and there's no way I could ever top you. But in honor of the late great George Carlin, I do want to leave you all with another seven words you will never hear on television, '. . . and the Emmy goes to Bob Saget.'"

With a closer like that, there's nothing left to do but take a bow and let the next person try to follow you. As they say in the roast business, always leave them wanting more.

• PROPS

If you're afraid of speaking in public, don't worry, you can still be a roaster. Using props allows you to talk less and let the jokes speak for themselves. Even yours truly, a guy who failed shop class three times, has a love for prop building. In fact, I was the one who told Carrot Top to attach a tiny key to a large black dildo and say that he found Lisa Lampanelli's car keys. Prop comics may not have to talk the talk—but they do have to top the Top.

• COSTUMES

I'm a very strong believer in artistic expression through wardrobe. Try dressing up as your guest of honor's priest, mom, or parole officer. The goal is to make your outfit part of your act. A minute into my roasting of Larry the Cable Guy, I ripped the arms off my tuxedo as an homage to the Git-R-Done guy's signature sleeveless style and yelled, "Git-R-Roasted!"

At Carson Daly's rock-and-roll "Bash" on MTV, I came out in a giant pink furry phallus costume and performed as Carson's penis. My opening joke was, "Look how relieved Kid Rock is that for once he's not the biggest dick in the room."

At Pam Anderson's roast, a few people booed when I walked in wearing a fur coat. I feigned confusion . . . "What? This is a benefit for PETA, right? People Who Eat and Torture Animals?"

I tagged it up with, "Don't worry, it's not real. We just shaved Bea Arthur's back."

This last example is interesting because not only is it a "tag," it's also a "twofer." Even though the joke was said to Pam Anderson, it was really about Bea Arthur. Once you start turning your "tags" into "twofers," then you have truly mastered the mysterious craft of writing roast jokes.

These are just a few of my secret techniques. However, there are infinite possibilities for ways of making fun of people, so don't hold back.

A ROASTMASTER MUST BE ABLE TO DEFEND HIMSELF

WHEN I WAS SIX YEARS old my mom enrolled me in The House of Empty Hands Karate School in Maplewood, New Jersey. Personally, I would have rather just sat around picking my nose and watching *The Jetsons*. But since my ghetto grade school didn't offer gym class and my mama was determined not to let me become a complete mama's boy, she dragged me there two afternoons a week against my will.

At first, I was so uncoordinated that I threw my forward punches upside down with my wrists facing the ceiling. But my mom made me stick with it and I eventually advanced to yellow belt. This inspired me to start practicing every day after school—mostly on my sister, who was very resilient. By the time I got my green belt I had the fastest feet in the dojo and I decided I wanted to be the Jewish Chuck Norris (rather, the *more* Jewish Chuck Norris).

After class my dad would usually pick me up and take me to the Burger King next door for a milk shake and we would dis-

cuss that night's performance. Like a boxer or a baseball pitcher, a martial artist thrives in the spotlight alone, while others watch and cheer. I think this solo dynamic is initially what attracted me to stand-up and roasting later on in life.

I also came to appreciate the value of discipline that karate teaches. Not only must you respect your teachers but your opponents as well. However, one time my mom tried to slap me for mouthing off and I instinctively deflected it with an outside block that broke her left pinkie. She was so impressed with the return on her investment that she didn't even punish me. I was quickly becoming the real-life Karate Kid. Practicing my kicks and katas every single day taught me how hard one must work to be the very best at something. Plus, I came to idolize my sensei, Master Ronnie Rosselli, a local Newark police detective with a thick moustache and a way with the ladies. It was he who first told me that I had natural abilities as a martial artist.

By the time I was nine, I had earned my brown belt and was now teaching Tae Kwon Do–style karate to other kids almost every day after school. I also had a shelf full of trophies and could pull off some impressive maneuvers with a pair of nunchucks. At the age of ten and a half, I had passed a yearlong test to become the second-youngest black belt in the country. To celebrate, my dad invited all of my friends and Little League teammates to a big black belt bash at his catering hall. Everybody we knew stuffed themselves with prime rib as I lit my nunchucks on fire on the center of the dance floor. Then after demonstrating a few impressive katas with my friend Lyle and breaking some boards with my bare hands, I thanked my parents for the best night of my life. After that I chopped a large chocolate sheet cake in half and everybody had dessert.

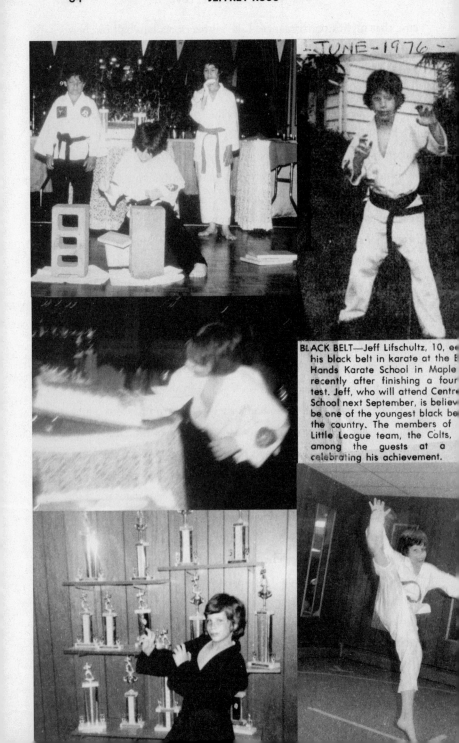

JUNE-1976-

BLACK BELT—Jeff Lifschultz, 10, ea
his black belt in karate at the B
Hands Karate School in Maple
recently after finishing a four
test. Jeff, who will attend Centr
School next September, is believ
be one of the youngest black be
the country. The members of
Little League team, the Colts,
among the guests at a
celebrating his achievement.

I sincerely believe that learning self-defense as a child gave me the self-confidence to mock people as an adult. That's why I highly recommend aspiring Roastmasters to learn how to protect themselves from poor sports. One time, at a roast for the Maloof brothers at their Palms Casino in Las Vegas, a belligerent Penny Marshall came charging toward me after I asked her to remind me "which character she played on *Laverne and Shirley,* again— Lenny or Squiggy?" Apparently, she was still mad at me for the time I roasted her ex-husband Rob Reiner when I opened up by saying, "Folks, how do you even embarrass a guy who married Penny Marshall? What was your wedding song, 'How Much Is That Doggy in the Window?' "

As the respected director of *A League of Their Own* lunged at me, I didn't even flinch. Although it probably would have been a close fight, I stood there with the confidence of knowing I could totally kick her ass if I really had to.

My background in self-defense also gives me the swagger to occasionally go on the comedic offense when necessary. Once when I was a guest cohost on *Jimmy Kimmel Live,* I found myself sitting next to imposing gangster and Death Row Records CEO Suge Knight. This was his first public appearance since being released from prison.

Although Jimmy was wearing a bulletproof vest over his suit, I was armed with nothing but attitude. Just to mess with Suge, I played dumb and acted like I had no idea who he was.

"I don't follow sports. I don't know what team you're on or anything. But you seem like a good guy." Suge laughed but for all I know he could have been laughing about how funny it would be when he strangled me later. After all, this is the guy who was rumored to have dangled Vanilla Ice off a balcony by his ankles.

Toward the end of the broadcast, we were escorted to Jimmy's outdoor stage to watch a performance by Suge's newest protégé, Crooked Eye. Just as Jimmy was about to introduce the song, Suge ripped the mic out of Jimmy's hands and gave shout-outs to all his homeys still on lockdown. Not wanting to see Jimmy disrespected like that during his first month on the air, I courageously grabbed the mic from Suge's hand and gave a shout-out to my rabbi back in Jersey, before handing it back over to Jimmy, who gracefully closed the show. It was great TV, but afterward, Jimmy was so worried about my safety that he had two security guards walk me to my car. I wasn't concerned at all. A Roastmaster must be fearless.

A ROASTMASTER MUST VISIT NEW JERSEY

$\mathcal{S}$ PENDING TIME IN DIRTY JERSEY is an essential part of any Roastmaster's training. After all, it's easier to talk trash when you're surrounded by it. But, contrary to popular belief, my home state is a breeding ground for more than just bacteria. The harsh environment also cultivates a brutal honesty among its native sons of bitches. It's virtually impossible to arrive in the land of Springsteen, Sinatra, and *The Sopranos* and pretend that you're anywhere else. The people, the accents, the music, the smell, the attitudes, the smell, the mannerisms, the odor, the architecture, and the stench—something will eventually remind you that you're in our nation's urinal.

We call our birthplace the

Garden State, which is a nice way to say the place smells like fertilizer. Our state bird is a falcon holding its beak. But eventually you adapt. By the time I was nine I had learned to breathe through my eyes. Nowadays, whenever I come home, all my old friends visit me—my aunts, my uncles, my eczema. . . .

During World War II, Mean Murray served in General Patton's army and even helped liberate one of the concentration camps. The experience gave him a fearless swagger. During the Newark riots he stood on the steps of our family catering hall protecting it with a shotgun. Mean Murray has really seen it all— and he understands better than anybody that a little ball busting is good for the soul.

Of course us Jerseyites aren't afraid to tell it like it is, even if somebody gets pissed off and slugs us in the kisser. In fact, that's exactly what happened to Great-Grandma Rosie, the renowned caterer, after she told a rude and unattractive bride and groom that they were both *so ugly their family pictures would hang themselves*. Of course, no one is safe from ridicule around here—not even family. Just recently I heard my uncle Murray refer to his granddaughters as "the looker and the cooker."

When I was a little kid, Uncle Murray, or, as he is known in the family, "Mean Murray," would constantly tease me about everything from the size of my teeth to the length of my hair. I used to really hate him for it and once I didn't talk to him for six straight months. I only forgave him because he poisoned another family member's Doberman pinscher after it bit my sister on the face. As I got older I learned to realize that my uncle Murray really did have a good heart, and that he was constantly kidding me because he loved me. In fact, he was making me a stronger person by teaching me something very important: how to take a joke.

As you can probably tell, I have a lot of affection for my deep Jersey roots. My family's catering business was once the most respected in the state. Author Judy Blume even wrote in her best seller *Wifey* that when she was growing up it was every girl's dream to one day meet a great guy and have a big wedding at Clinton Manor Caterers in Newark. Plus, Bruce Springsteen's very own E Street Band–mate, drummer Max Weinberg, is my second cousin. Trust me, you can't get any more Jersey than that without catching a lung infection.

Not only do I think Max is one of the best drummers in the world, but watching him perform live with the E Street Band

"BORN TO RUN" MEETS BORN TO ROAST: ME AND MIGHTY MAX CHILLIN' AT OUR COUSIN JOSH'S BAR MITZVAH.

offers us a lesson in showmanship. Although he is onstage for almost three hours with Springsteen every night they perform, Max somehow manages to end each concert with just a little more energy than he starts it with. In fact, when "The Boss" introduces "Mighty Max" at the end of a show he often uses the word *unstoppable*.

The lesson here is: Start strong and finish stronger. In a way, Bruce Springsteen's whole show builds to the last song. When John Stamos took Bob Saget and me to see them live in Los Angeles recently, they closed with the Jersey Shore anthem, "Rosalita." I hadn't heard that song live in years, so I couldn't help but take my shirt off and go completely berserk—at least until a security guard came over and demanded I put it back on. You can take the boy out of Jersey, but you can't take the Jersey out of the boy.

First stop for those visiting is usually Newark International—the only airport with graffiti on the sides of the planes. Trust me, air travel is fun again when you're flying with Jet Blue Balls or Cuntinental. Last time I was there I got patted down three times. And that was just in the men's room. When I finally got to the actual security checkpoint, I couldn't help but notice that the guard wanding me had all gold teeth. The buzzer kept going off. Finally I said, "I think it's you, man." Despite all these precautions, I still found a homeless guy eating peanuts in my overhead compartment.

Surely spending some quality time in the wisecrack capital of the world will whet your sense of insult humor. After all, we are the state whose governor proudly declared to his constituents that he was a "gay American" before he even told his wife and kids. Then his replacement nearly died in a car crash because he refused to wear a seat belt while his motorcade sped down the Garden State Parkway at 91 miles an hour. Was he headed to a big cabinet meeting? Was he responding to a state emergency? Sort of, I guess. . . . He was racing to meet with disc jockey Don Imus, who had just called the Rutgers University women's basketball team a bunch of "nappy-headed hos." Bada-Bing! Fuhgedaboutit! Around here, disses cut deep.

But that's okay—we can take it. In fact, Jersey itself was the recipient of perhaps the harshest insult in mankind's history. Everyone in the world remembers that miraculous day when large birds knocked out both engines of U.S. Air's Flight 1549 en route from New York to North Carolina. Remember the cockpit recording between air traffic control and Captain Chesley "Sully" Sullenberger? "Captain, we have a clear runway at Teterboro Airport in New Jersey. . . ." "Fuck that! I'm going in the water! Brace for impact!"

Upon your arrival, you may want to observe the natives from a distance. Don't worry, we're easy to spot. At two thousand Jerseyites per square mile, we are the densest state in the union. The fact that we're all up in one another's business explains our constant shoulder shrugging and neck bobbing. Jerseyites have a unique way of walking—we zigzag so as to avoid the odors and garbage that prey on us in our natural habitat. You'll also notice we have a certain way of talking, one that is spiked with imaginative expletives and punctuated by loud belches and hacking fits. And that's just the children. In fact, I have two very funny nephews. Their names are Mitchell and Jared and they're like a little comedy team. I call them The Jeffews. One is going to be a lawyer. One is going to need a lawyer.

HERE JARED AND I ARE ATTEMPTING TO PISS OFF HIS GRANDMOTHER BY REMOVING OUR SHIRTS DURING THANKSGIVING DINNER. IN FACT, GIVING THANKS BY GETTING NAKED IS BECOMING A TRADITION IN OUR WHACKED-OUT FAMILY.

Li'l Jared loves to make up funny songs and tell Mexican jokes. He already understands that making fun of people is an art form. Recently his third grade class had to write some funny lyrics about their teacher, Mrs. Evans, for a school music recital. One student questioned whether the joke about her being "older than math" might offend Mrs. Evans. Jared politely explained to his classmate that "the old goat" was old enough to take a joke and should be honored by it. Clearly my nephew is showing early signs of Roastmastery.

Personally I don't remember zinging my way in or out of trouble until shortly before my tenth birthday. One day after school, my friends and I were playing a heated game of four-on-four, shirts versus skins basketball in the Antonelli brothers' backyard.

The game was tied—triple overtime and somehow I got hold of the ball and had an open shot. My teammates shouted, "Shoot! Shoot!" But I didn't dare. Previously whenever I tried to sink a shot from that far out I'd either get completely stuffed or launch it over the backboard into the next yard. The kid guarding me, Dale Wirkus, took a step back hoping I'd do just that. But I didn't shoot the ball. Instead, I just stood there paralyzed in my Pumas. I looked to my left—nowhere to go. I looked to my right. Nobody open. Again, my teammates yelled, "Shoot! Shoot! Shooooot!" At that point I just dropped the ball, pointed my finger like a pistol, and aimed it at each of them as I said, "Bang! Bang! Bang!" Suddenly seven seven-year-olds fell on the ground laughing so hard that it didn't matter who won the game. Whether on a court or a dais, timing really is everything. When openings present themselves, don't hesitate. Just say it.

I also believe that growing up in my family's multicultural catering hall further cultivated my already natural inclination to be an equal opportunity offender. Unlike, say, Nebraskans or Puerto Ricans, Jerseyites don't all look alike. In fact, our strength and sense of humor come from our differences. Between the cranky Jewish chef, the inebriated Scottish, Irish, and English waitresses, the stoned Haitian dishwashers, the horny Danish hat-check girl, the erudite Russian fruit cup maker, and Lester the Hungarian pastry chef, who liked to show me naked pictures of his obese girlfriend, I got a well-rounded gawk at mankind from an early age.

However, it wasn't until I reached Jonathan Dayton Regional High School in Springfield that I discovered the great power of the put-down. Our school bully, Joe Sefack, was a big hairy manboy with an oversize forehead. This talking ape was twice the size of everybody else and would lurk in the dark corners of the hallways. Then when you least expected it, he would LEAP out of the shadows and WHACK people in the DICK with his FIST as HARD as he could. Then he'd stand there laughing like an intoxicated moose as his target lay in pain.

On more than one occasion, even I, the second-youngest black belt in the country, fell victim to this merciless genital terrorism. Not only were these attacks extremely humiliating, I strongly believe they caused permanent damage to the size of my manhood, which hasn't grown much since boyhood. Either way, this guy was a real schmuck who needed to be put in his place.

I decided the next time he whacked me I would try to shake it off and use my martial arts training to kick his ass. But then I witnessed him break another kid's wrist because he cut in front of him on the lunch line. I decided that a physical confrontation with this psychopath was not my best path to revenge. Instead, I snuck out to the parking lot during class and dragged a sharp key along the side of his new Trans Am. Of course, my cowardly vandalism gave me more guilt than satisfaction, and Sefack continued his agonizing assaults.

Besides sharing two classes, I also played on the high school football team with this Cro-Magnon maniac, and he would often pull the same crap in the locker room. One of our teammates would be heading off to the showers wearing nothing but a towel, and then BAM—Sefack would leap out of a locker and punch him as hard as he could right in the penis area. Of course, none of us ever came to anybody else's defense out of fear of being the next victim. With teamwork like that it's hard to believe we didn't win a game in two seasons.

One night after a long practice, Sefack snuck up behind me

and slugged me extremely hard in my extremities for no reason whatsoever. As I lay on the locker room floor holding my junk together, something weird and dangerous and magical took over inside me. I started to speak through the tears . . . "Fuck you, Sefack—you ugly hairy bastard. You're like Chewbacca's retarded cousin."

Everybody on the team laughed. Sefack's face contorted. This made me feel a little better, so I kept going, "You fucking ugly ass-hole. The last time I saw a face like yours it was catching a Frisbee in its mouth." The more we laughed, the more he cowered. Sefack never punched me in the crotch again—and a young insult comic was born.

Yes, Jersey boys and girls sure are a brash bunch. In fact, if I were ever to open an Academy of Roasting, there would be no other state in the union I would even consider breaking ground in. This is partly because of some gambling debts I have with some "construction contractors" in East Orange, but it's also because New Jersey is teeming with the kind of raw humanity that opens your eyes to the infinite ways of making fun of people. In New Jersey, everybody's a Roastmaster.

ROASTING A JERSEY PAISAN

Although Jerseyites are tough on the outside, we are often sensitive on the inside. In fact, I once made the respected actor, singer, and Italian-American icon Danny Aiello cry. It happened when I roasted the longtime Saddle River resident shortly after the debut of his new television detective show, *Dellaventura*. Not only did every critic in the country pan the show, so did every comedian on the dais that day.

I started off by reading a mock ransom note that went roughly like this, "Danny Aiello is my favorite actor—or else." Then I launched into a barrage of jokes playing off his movie gangster persona:

"Contrary to popular belief, Danny Aiello does not have friends in the mob. He has relatives in the mob. But what can you really say about Danny Aiello that hasn't already been said by some guy in the Witness Protection Program with nine fingers? Danny, I really hope your next show is successful, 'cause let's face it—you haven't had a hit since that bank job in '79. All kidding aside, the only crime Danny is guilty of is his acting in *Dellaventura*. That performance was so over the top they should've replaced him with Jim Carrey and called it *Ace Dellaventura*."

At this point I finally looked over at the guest of honor. Tears were steaming down his cheeks. I wasn't sure if they were tears of joy or sorrow—or if he had simply caught a whiff of Richard Belzer's breath—so I continued. . . .

"And Danny, after I watched your TV miniseries about a family of gangsters called *The Last Don*, three words came to mind, 'Let's hope so.' There were even rumors that Danny might win an Emmy for his work playing a mobster in that movie. Folks, Danny Aiello getting an Emmy for playing a mobster would be like Eddie Murphy getting an Emmy for playing a black guy."

Suddenly I heard a weird gasp from the crowd. I looked toward Danny. His chair was empty. He was gone! I froze. I didn't know what to do. He had disappeared backstage to either pee or order a hit on me. But I wasn't finished with my jokes. Suddenly the Dean of the New York Friars Club, Freddie Roman, ran over, sat in Danny's chair, and put on Danny's sunglasses. With no reasonable alternative, I began roasting Freddie *as* Danny.

"Danny, of course I'm a big fan. Especially of the project you are working on right at this very second! Wow, folks. You should've seen all the press backstage . . . thirty reporters, twenty television crews, and three sketch artists. Of course, Danny's acting has won prizes at all the major festivals—including San Gennaro and the Feast of St. Anthony's.

"Anyway, to research this roast I asked Danny's parole officer—I mean publicist—to send me Danny's extensive rap sheet—I mean, résumé. There are so many projects Danny has done that most of us have long forgotten about—such as the wonderful Sicilian soap opera he starred in titled *One Life to Live with Sentences to Run Consecutively.* Not to mention the hit game show he hosted called *Let's Make a Deal You Can't Refuse.*"

Finally, the actual Danny Aiello came back just as I pulled a giant boom box from underneath the podium. I hit Play and the theme from *The Godfather* started filling the room. Everybody there knew that this was the first movie Danny ever appeared in. Then my old pal (literally) Abe Vigoda appeared from backstage as an homage to his classic role as Tessio in the film.

He said, "Jeff! Jeff! I have an urgent message from the Godfather!" I took the note and said, "Thank you, Tessio." The audience burst into applause out of respect for Abe. He smiled and took a bow. Then I pretended to read the note. "Oh! This is great news, everybody! Great news! Danny, this is so kind of you. It says because I did this roast today the Mafia's gonna release my family!" I leaned over and kissed Danny, who was finally laughing through his tears.

Afterward, Danny told me that he cried not because the jokes hurt his feelings, but because he was sad that his dad had not lived long enough to see him receive the honor of a Friars Club roast. Next time you're passing through Hoboken, stop into his Danny's Upstairs nightclub on Washington Street and bust his balls for me. I know for a fact he can take it, because he's a Jersey boy.

THE FRIARS' FIRST-EVER ROASTMISTRESS JOY BEHAR, ME, AND FREDDIE ROMAN, WHO IS PRETENDING TO BE DANNY AIELLO.

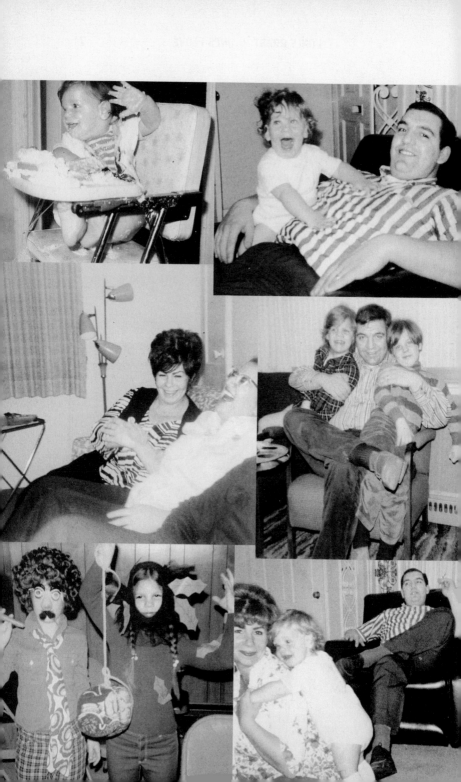

A ROASTMASTER
HAS IT IN HIS BLOOD

*I*F YOU'RE A BONA FIDE Roastmaster, funny probably runs in your family. My mom had a bawdy sense of humor and was my very first fan. In fact, any time anybody said something funny, Marsha Lifschultz was the first one to bust a gut laughing and fall on the floor.

Unfortunately, I was only twelve years old when she got sick. During that time my sister, Robyn, and I learned to look out for ourselves. We did our own laundry and unclogged our own toilets. While my mom was away at the hospital for long periods of time, it wasn't uncommon for me to eat two bowls of Frosted Flakes for dinner, do some homework, and go to bed. I never complained or felt sorry for myself. This was just life as I knew it.

I remember my dad taking my little sister and me into New York to visit my mom at Sloan-Kettering Hospital whenever possible. On one occasion my mom was particularly sad and self-conscious because chemotherapy had caused all her hair to fall out. By coincidence my sister and I had just come from seeing the bald actor Yul Brynner on Broadway in *The King and I*. Before long the cue ball jokes began flowing and by the time visiting hours were over our mom was laughing again.

A few days before Mother's Day, my dad came home from work early and called my sister and me into the den. He put his big arms around us and said, "Mommy passed away today." I wasn't surprised at all. In fact, after two years of worrying about her I was kind of relieved.

This painful time made me appreciate my dad a lot more than I ever had before. After all, we had a lot in common. We were both single. We both loved to gamble. And we both ate like animals. It was a family tradition to stuff ourselves at a Chinese restaurant and then stop and pick up a pizza on the way home.

One afternoon I came home from school and my dad crank-

ily said, "Go clean up your room." I went to my bedroom and found a shiny new silver-and-black moped with a red ribbon tied around the seat. My dad stood there laughing. He told me he was tired of driving me around.

Not only was my dad my best friend, he was also the funniest guy I knew. When I was about twelve he paid me to run naked around the backyard during a snowstorm. He once dared my sister to sit on the curb in a scarf and coat for an hour during a heat wave. Of course, both times he locked us out of the house for an extra few minutes just to make the whole stunt even more hilarious.

Late one Saturday night, he came home from the catering hall still wearing his work tux. My high school pals and I were sitting around the kitchen table playing poker. My lifelong buddy Howard "Haimo" Haimowitz had already lost fifty bucks, which was a lot of money for an eleventh grader with a fledgling car

**MY HIGH SCHOOL BUDDIES PLAYING POKER IN MY KITCHEN.
THAT'S HAIMO ON THE RIGHT.**

waxing business to blow back then. When Haimo lost yet another big pot, my dad whipped out a hundred-dollar bill and slapped it down on the table. "Haimo, I got a proposition for you!" Haimo's eyes widened as my dad went over to the fridge and took out a stick of butter. "If you eat this entire stick in less than five minutes, you can keep that money," my dad said as he tossed the stick of butter over to him.

Of course, we all encouraged Haimo to go for it. Not only would that C-note make him even for the night, but he'd have enough money left over to see Bruce Springsteen play at Giants Stadium later that summer. On the other hand, Haimo had a sensitive stomach and this stunt could not possibly end well.

After much contemplation, Haimo finally accepted the dare and began unwrapping the Land O'Lakes. My dad jokingly tossed him a tiny scrap of bread to go with it. As Haimo took his first big bite of butter, his face contorted and his eyes immediately started watering. Each little nibble after that nearly did him in. When he had the stick of butter about halfway down, his stomach finally backfired. Haimo stumbled over to the kitchen sink and puked his guts out. When we were all done laughing our asses off, my dad let him keep the money. He'd earned it.

I get my equal opportunity offensiveness from my dad. His dares and pranks weren't reserved just for friends and family. Years later, while on a weekend getaway to Atlantic City with his new girlfriend Barbara, my dad spotted his favorite comic, Don Rickles, eating dinner in the same restaurant. Rather than just be another guy asking for an autograph, he decided to impress his girlfriend by re-creating a famous prank Don Rickles once pulled on Frank Sinatra at the Sands in Vegas.

My dad carefully approached the legend's table and said, "Mr.

Rickles, I don't mean to bother you, but my name is Ronny Lifschultz. I'm on a big date tonight with a woman I really care about and it would mean the world to us if you just walked by the table and said hello, like you know me. I know she'll get a huge kick out of it, and so will I."

"Okay. Sure, no problem," Mr. Rickles said. "What's her name?"

"Her name is Barbara," my dad answered excitedly.

Believe it or not, about ten minutes later, Don Rickles approached my dad's table with a smile on his face and arms opened wide. "Hey, Ronny! How you doing?" he said warmly. "Is this Barbara—the new lady that I've heard so much about?"

With perfect timing, my dad dropped his fork, looked up, and deadpanned, "Don, can't you see we're eating?" With that, all three of them cracked up. What an incredible moment for my dad. He had done what few have ever dared to attempt: he busted the balls of the King of Insult Comics with the same practical joke Rickles had pulled on Sinatra.

Everybody in Union County knew my dad. Although he took his work very seriously, my dad did like to mess around with the customers just to keep things loose and festive. If there was a guest he knew well, he would jokingly serve their prime rib using his bare hands. Like a true Roastmaster, he was able to pull off being silly even in the most formal of settings.

After my dad shipped me off to study film at Boston University, he started sending me a small allowance every week. But I sent it back and got a job as a short-order cook at Charlie's Cafeteria Deli in Kenmore Square. It wasn't always fun working from ten at night to six in the morning making western omelets for cranky cabbies, but I wanted my dad to understand that I appreciated

him—and that paying my college tuition was enough. More than anything, I just wanted him to be proud of me.

College was my first full-fledged foray into artistic indulgence. On Friday nights I hosted a punk rock comedy show called *Wipe-out* with my new pals Mark and Dosage on WTBU, our student-run radio station. On Tuesday afternoons I played rhythm guitar with a couple of tattooed townies in a rockabilly ensemble we called the High Gear Daddies. Then at midnight on Saturdays I acted out the role of Frank-N-Furter, the "sweet transvestite" from *The Rocky Horror Picture Show,* at the Exeter Street Theater downtown. That's right, folks—my first live performing experience was dancing around in high heels and fishnets in front of a movie screen. Despite getting a B-minus in chemistry, I was having the time of my life.

Then one morning during my sophomore year, I got a call from my Pop Jack saying he found my dad passed out on his bedroom floor. He said I should come home right away. My cousin Aron picked me up at the airport and broke down sobbing. Nothing he said was making sense. He couldn't bear to tell me what I had to see for myself.

When we got to the hospital, I found my dad unconscious and breathing hard. Two long days and nights later, he was dead of a cerebral hemorrhage.

His funeral was a blur. I gave a eulogy but I don't remember it. I do recall finally laughing with my sister when her dog started humping the rabbi's leg in our living room during the memorial service. I also remember my cousin Tracy getting me drunk after the funeral and piercing my ear with a needle and an apple.

And of course, I'll never forget fooling around with my voluptuous neighbor Gabrielle that very night. I had a crush on her all through high school, and afterward I remember thinking how much I wished I could've told my dad all about it.

This intense period was sad, surreal, and liberating all at the same time. My sister was eighteen, I was nineteen—and we were suddenly on our own. When our relatives and neighbors offered to adopt us, we had trouble keeping a straight face. Nobody was going to hold us down. Two months later, I was backpacking through Europe with a buddy.

It's my belief that we as humans are built to mourn—and then move on. I've never spent much time feeling sorry for myself. I believe a Roastmaster must respect the past but not dwell on it. Winners think about tomorrow. Everything in life can be taken away from you except your experiences. Therefore, a Roastmaster should never feel like a victim, because everything that happens to you eventually makes you funnier. Being a Roastmaster is a life paved with broken hearts and busted balls and you must be able to confront it all with a positive attitude.

My mentor Buddy Hackett once told me, "Comedians feel pain more than regular people because that's our trade. We don't sell cars or fabric; we sell our emotions." This is why a Roastmaster must swallow his sorrow and transform it into humor. The sadder the subject, the bigger the laughs.

I never could have predicted or planned the life I have now. Surely, if my folks hadn't passed away I might never have become a comedian. I probably would've wound up being the second-funniest kosher caterer in New Jersey. Still, I can't help but wonder how much more fun my journey as The Roastmaster General would have been with my parents cheering me on from the front row.

I recently shot a big stand-up special back home in New Jersey. On my way down to Atlantic City, I stopped by the cemetery where my parents are buried. Once again I thought about what a great laugher my mom was and how funny my dad could be. I also thought about how hard my dad worked so I could go to Boston University, and about how my mom dragged me to that karate school against my will. It's as if they were preparing me to take care of myself after they were gone. Luckily that martial arts training made me just flexible enough to pat myself on the back once in a while. I miss my parents, but through it all, a Roastmaster must be okay on his own.

AMATEUR HOUR

"I don't understand tolltakers . . . I mean, how fulfilling can that job be? Any job that when you call in sick they just replace you with a basket."

"When you're born and raised in New Jersey you become immune to the stench. . . . I'm on the Jersey Turnpike the other day with my friend who's not from Jersey and he's like [SNIFF], 'What the hell is that? Toxic waste? Garbage?' I'm like [SNIFF], 'Waffles!' "

"On Halloween I forgot to buy candy for the kids . . . the doorbell rang . . . I panicked . . . so I gave 'em all cigarettes."

"This is a love poem. It's called 'I Miss Her Sometimes.' I ran into my old girlfriend recently. Then I backed up and ran into her again. I miss her sometimes."

A ROASTMASTER ONLY STARTS OUT ONCE

*P*EOPLE ALWAYS ASK ME HOW I got my start in comedy. The truth is I took a beginner's class in stand-up by accident. Originally I thought it was a writing class, but it turned out that my good pal Mark Chapin had tricked me into taking it because I always cracked him up. At the time, I was a chubby guy two years out of college with very little money and no social life whatsoever. Plus Epitome Productions, the corporate video company I started with my college pal Brian Weiner, was on the brink of filing Chapter 11 for the eleventh time. Basically, I was a loser living in New Jersey with my grandfather. At the very least, I figured taking a stand-up comedy class in the city one night a week might be a good way to meet chicks. It wasn't. But it was a great way to meet my destiny.

The teacher was a funny guy named Lee Frank, who taught us not only the basics—like how to remove the mic from the stand

and then place the stand behind you so it's out of your way—but also more philosophical concepts such as, "If it doesn't offend somebody somewhere, it's not a joke." Regardless, the very idea of saying whatever I wanted on a stage into a microphone under a spotlight in front of total strangers seemed rather enticing. Growing up, my favorite comics were Eddie Murphy, Cheech and Chong, the Blues Brothers, and Steve Martin. But I didn't think of them as comedians. I thought of them as rock stars just like Elvis Costello or The Clash. Taking this introductory class helped me understand that comics are just regular people who see the world a little differently. I decided I fit that description and dived into the course.

One of our first assignments was to tell a painful story without being funny. I talked about getting busted for smoking pot behind the Dumpster at my dad's catering hall with Cold Duck Eddie Green, the head dishwasher. I don't remember the story but I do remember getting a lot of unintended laughs just by laying out the facts. Suddenly I had academic proof that I was a naturally funny person. Like most aspiring Roastmasters, I simply had to fail at more traditional endeavors such as business and romance before discovering what I was really good at.

The class met for three hours on Tuesday nights in a small classroom inside a run-down theater on the same block as the Port Authority Bus Terminal. This was very convenient because I lived an hour away by bus in Springfield, New Jersey, with my mom's dad, Pop Jack. Even when times were tough, he could always cheer me up just by making a joke or calling me by his nickname for me, which was "Champ."

Pop and I were inseparable. We shared each other's clothes and ate most of our meals together at a nearby diner on Route

22. Occasionally he would peer out the diner window over to our bank across the highway and say, "Hey, Champ, does the door over there look locked? I got almost three hundred bucks stashed in that place and I don't want nobody breakin' in."

Pop Jack had a soft deep voice like a blues singer, big thick hands like catchers' mitts, and sweet bulging eyes like E.T., the extraterrestrial. All the old widows at the senior center had the hots for him because he could still see well enough to drive at night. I once asked him what actually happens when he makes love at his

age. "When you finish, does anything happened? Does anything come out?" Pop contemplated the question for a beat and said simply, "Insulin."

Not only was he diabetic but he also had angina, shingles, and cancer of the esophagus. I took him to all his doctor appointments and spent many days and nights with him at nearby Overlook Hospital. Even with all these ailments, Pop Jack never lost his sense of humor. Once when I was wheeling him out of his hospital room to take him home he looked back at the patient lying despondent in the bed next to his and said, "Hey, if I ain't back in four days go ahead and die without me. In the meantime, feel free to attack my leftover Jell-O." Another time when we were in a pharmacy to pick up his meds, he walked right up to the counter and said in a booming voice, "You got anything for ball rash? I got ball rash over here. My grandson's got it too! Show her, Champ!" Anybody who met him never forgot him. At his seventy-ninth birthday party he told everybody he was eighty because he knew he'd get better presents.

Still, as a retired construction foreman from the Bronx, it was hard for him to wrap his mind around my wanting to tell jokes for a living. After all, I was his first descendant to graduate college and now I was throwing it all away to try stand-up comedy. But he supported me anyway. Each time I left the house in search of stage time in the city, Pop Jack would give me a few bucks for the tolls and a ripe banana in case of a hunger emergency. "Take a banana for the ride," he'd always say.

So with a tape recorder in my pocket and a banana on the seat next to me, I would hop into the white Jeep Wrangler my sister bought me with her settlement money from a drunk driving accident and drive through the Holland Tunnel to Manhattan and

do as many as seven shows a night. The latest I ever went on was 4:50 a.m. at the Improv in Hell's Kitchen in front of a bunch of drunken kids in tuxedos and gowns, who had just come from their senior prom. It was my job to entertain them as they tried to get hand jobs under the table. Still, I managed to crush with jokes I'm no longer proud of, such as, "I couldn't get a date for my prom so I took my cousin. His name's Anthony. But hey, at least I got laid."

Back then there were two kinds of comics among my peers—those who traveled all the time and were considered crowd-pleasing "road acts," and those who aspired to be edgier and more sophisticated "city acts." I was determined to be both. Whenever I wasn't making a few hundred bucks at Wiseguys in Syracuse or Coconuts in Boca Raton, I would be in New York City popping into the showcase clubs to earn twenty bucks for twenty minutes.

Before I could move up to better spots, I had to pay my dues by being the weekend "backup." This meant I got twenty bucks a show to sit around Catch A Rising Star all night, hoping one of the big shots got hit by a bus so I could go onstage and make an extra thirty bucks. Since there were two shows Friday and three on Saturday, I was guaranteed a whopping one hundred bucks for the weekend whether I got my shot or not.

Late one Friday night, my prayers were answered when Mario Joyner's car got stuck in the snow. On sixty seconds' notice, I took a leak and jumped onstage to close out a show that included Colin Quinn, David Brenner, Bill Hicks, and Jerry Seinfeld. Patrons noisily paid their checks while I quietly bombed for ten minutes. Afterward, I drove back to Jersey eating a banana, wondering what the hell I was doing with my life.

Eventually, Pop Jack's health fell apart. His body was losing so much blood he became weak and began to hallucinate. Once I came home after a late set and found him sitting in the living room with socks on his hands mumbling incoherently about General Noriega being in the basement with guns. It seems that everybody in life is twice a child—once when they're young, and once when they're old. Toward the end, Pop Jack would stumble into my room late at night and lie across the bottom of my bed. Then he would hold on to my foot or ankle and sleep that way until morning. Finally one afternoon, I carried him to my jeep and drove him to the hospital, where he died.

An hour later, I removed the ring from his thick middle finger as he had instructed me to do. It was actually a steel bolt from a Nazi submarine that he sanded into a ring during his days serving with the U.S. Coast Guard during World War II. I put it on and have never taken it off.

A few days later, the talent coordinator at Catch A Rising Star, Louis Faranda, told me that since I no longer had to take care of anybody else I should now devote myself to becoming a full-time comedian. That was just the pep talk I needed to corroborate my already burning desire to get onstage as much as humanly possible.

One night I was running late for my backup spot, so I double-parked in front of the club. The first act hadn't shown up either so I had to go right onstage and fill time. After my set, I came outside and discovered that my Jeep had been smashed into by a hit-and-run driver. The hood was smoking, it had a huge dent, and one of the tires was flat. Without that means of transportation, I was no longer a professional comedian. I couldn't talk or even think straight. Like a stranded little orphan, I just wanted to stand in the street and cry.

Suddenly a Jewish angel named Jon Stewart appeared over my shoulder. He'd seen everything through the window of the club.

He told me to relax and he flagged down a cop. After helping me fill out the police report, he borrowed another comedian's AAA card and got me and my wrecked Wrangler a free tow back to my mechanic in Jersey.

I hardly knew Jon Stewart and his kindness meant even more considering he was my favorite act to watch during my back-up nights. Of course, Jon Stewart wasn't yet an American icon—he was just a brash Jersey boy who wore the same jean jacket every night and had such control over his crowds that he would kill even as he lay on the dirty stage doing his act to the ceiling. He would riff and scream about race and religion and politics and even about his cat getting neutered in a way that no other regular city act had the balls to do. In fact, I once saw a guy take a swing at him from the front row because he didn't agree with some joke Jon did about gays in the military. I admired the way Jon just didn't give a shit, standing up there in his dirty jean jacket.

One time he even let me open for him at a Jewish singles show. The crowd wasn't full of young Hebrew hotties like we were hoping, but rather it was packed with elderly, whiny widows who thrive on walking out on the entertainment. I went out there and bombed for fifteen minutes, but it didn't matter because to this old-world crowd, I was just a nice Jewish boy attempting to tell clean jokes while wearing a fancy blue sport jacket. I may not have gotten any laughs, but I didn't get any walkouts either. When I finally came off stage, I instinctively offered Jon my sport jacket. Without hesitation he put it on and said, "Wish me luck—I gotta do forty-five minutes for these fucking people." Without censoring or editing himself, Jon performed with confidence and let the stuck-up crowd come to him. Despite about a twenty percent walk-out rate, he killed and even earned the respect of those who stayed. Plus, I had learned a valuable lesson about the importance of committing to your material.

By the time the shows ended uptown at Catch, The Comic Strip, and Stand-up New York, things would just be getting started downtown. Sometimes there were more comics than customers in the audience, but the oddly named Boston Comedy Club on Third Street in Greenwich Village off Washington Square Park seemed to stay open until they ran out of comics, which was basically never.

The lengthy lineups were chock-full of fine stand-ups like Dave Attell, Rich Vos, Jim Norton, Jay Mohr, Wanda Sykes, Stu Kamens, Tony Woods, Patrice O'Neal, Tracy Morgan, Keith Robinson, Elon Gold, Bill Bellamy, D. C. Benny, Dane Cook, and the rapping duo of Red Johnny and the Round Guy—who were the first guys ever to hire me as their writer. If I got hungry waiting my turn I could always run around the corner to the Comedy Cellar on MacDougal Street and talk Manny, the benevolent dictator who owned the place, into letting me do a few minutes in exchange for one of those delicious falafel sandwiches he sold upstairs at the Olive Tree Cafe. Even after all that, the night wouldn't be complete until I played an early morning game of Scrabble in Louis C. K.'s filthy Bleecker Street apartment with Todd Barry and Sarah Silverman.

Even while she was still a student at New York University, Sarah was already a star in the eyes of us rookie comics. She is braver than most and never afraid to try anything in the name of experimentation. I once saw her sing, tap-dance, and finger herself all in the same set. Sarah's uncanny ability to play dumb and smart at the same time has made her one of the more prolific insultarians of our time. The first time I remember her really creaming somebody was when she said to a guy in the front row at the Boston Comedy Club, "Hey, you remind me of Rocky." The guy was flattered. Sarah went in for the kill. "Did you ever see that movie *Mask*?"

Back then, Sarah would warm up for her sets by walking up Third Street roasting every single homeless person. She knew all of their names and gave them all money even though she was borrowing from me. All the comics had crushes on her, but I always

FROM OUR EARLY DAYS AS STRUGGLING COMICS GETTING STONED IN MOVIE THEATER BATHROOMS TO FAMOUS COMICS LUNCHING IN BEVERLY HILLS, SARAH AND I HAVE BEEN FRIENDS FOR A LONG TIME. A ROASTMASTER SHOULD ALWAYS HAVE A PAL YOU CAN GET INTO SOME TROUBLE WITH.

considered her more of a sister than anything else. Not that I didn't realize how beautiful she is, but I knew she'd be my friend forever and I didn't want to mess it up by getting rejected in the back booth of the Boston Comedy Club.

One night a skinny, buck-toothed teenager from Washington, D.C., ambled in and talked Jason the manager into putting him on for five minutes. He looked about sixteen and told the audience that this was his first time in a comedy club without his mom. His name was Dave Chappelle and he cracked everybody up with a routine about how Batman would never try to fight crime in his tough neighborhood back in D.C. "Hey, Robin, didn't we park the Batmobile right here?"

Even though Dave was still about four pubes short of manhood, he already had a soft-spoken delivery and laid-back persona that went over big with the downtown crowd. Some of the regular city acts watching from the back rolled their eyes and figured somebody else must be writing his material. I was skeptical too, but willing to give this new kid the benefit of the doubt because he made me laugh so damn hard. After watching him kill for three nights straight, I was so impressed I offered to sneak him into Nell's on Fourteenth Street, where I bought him his first beer in the big city.

Afterward I took him on a driving tour of Manhattan while we listened to Arrested Development with the top down in my newly repaired Wrangler. Finally, at about 3 a.m., we pulled up to the Fulton Fish Market alongside the East River, which used to be all lit up at night like some sort of outdoor sturgeon stadium of stench. We leaned on my Jeep and talked until sunrise about fish and comedy and girls and life. Then I dropped him off at his new apartment on Washington Street in the West Village and drove my sleepy ass back to Jersey. The next night we did it all over again.

Eventually, Dave started getting booked at colleges around the East Coast and I was one of his regular openers. I would drive into the city, wake him up, and then we'd roll to wherever we were booked. I remember getting big applause with a joke about how expensive tuition was. "Remember when you were in high school . . . you'd get these college brochures filled with pictures of students, happy . . . smiling . . . having a book-covering party. You never see the kid in front of the financial aid office with a gun in his mouth. And his parents right behind him going, 'Do it! Do it! We could buy a boat!'"

I would do half an hour before bringing up Dave, who did a solid hour before closing with an elaborate bit about how he used to have the most dangerous job in Washington, D.C.: "I used to deliver pizzas for Domino's. They would rob me every day! I had to get a gun. I would bust into people's apartments—[kicking down door and pointing a gun] . . . Domino's, freeze! Put the money on the table! Now I'm gonna get out of here nice and slow . . . but first one of you motherfuckers is gonna have to tip me."

After one gig at the University of Pennsylvania, a kid from the student activities board got us stoned out of our minds. Like a scene out of Dave's eventual first film *Half Baked,* we were now two friends in a strange town besieged with the munchies. We jumped out of the kid's car and walked off toward a lit-up convenience store. In the back of the store was a cabinet of Dunkin' Donuts. As I headed toward it like a bug to a bulb, I was stopped in my tracks by the sight of an unusually overweight police officer with his entire upper body submerged inside the donut cabinet. This blob in blue was rummaging so diligently in search of his favorite variety that only his butt crack was visible—and you could've parked a bike in it.

Because I was not half but totally baked, I had to bite on my hand to keep from laughing. Chappelle was already at the register waiting to pay for his Dr Pepper and Twinkies. I walked over and not so discreetly pointed the corpulent copper out to him. When this officer of the law finally emerged from the cabinet with a French cruller in one hand, a jelly doughnut in the other, and a glazed apple fritter sticking out of his mouth, Dave and I lost our shit and flopped around on the floor like two Fulton fish out of water. The poor guy finally figured out we were laughing at him and nearly shot both of us in an attempt to regain his dignity.

Eventually I made the big move out of New Jersey and into a three-hundred-room mansion that I shared with five hundred other people on Mercer Street in Greenwich Village. My apartment was small, but my universe had suddenly expanded. I was closer to the comedy clubs and all my new funny friends. I was officially a city act.

It's common for comics to get together and waste an afternoon. One of my favorite spots to go for inspiration has always been Washington Square Park. Frequently I would meet up with Chappelle under the giant arch at the park's entrance. From there we would wander around smoking weed, eating hot pretzels with mustard, and talking to the NYU girls who sat in the park doing their homework.

It was also there that we came across a remarkable street performer named Charlie Barnett. Whenever the weather was nice, Charlie would hop up on a pillar in the middle of the park's empty fountain and just start yelling at the top of his lungs, "It's showtime! It's showtime, everybody!" Within minutes he would attract a diverse crowd of students, tourists, homeless people, as well as two young comics eager to watch and learn. It was always educational to see Charlie work the fountain like a true Roastmaster. He had an arsenal of one-liners that were too edgy for the indoor venues . . .

"I took an AIDS test—got a 65."

"Best thing about crack . . . brought the price of pussy down to five dollars."

"Hey, I'm not even black—this is a birthmark."

"If God didn't want man to eat pussy, why did he make it look like a taco?"

And whoever walked by automatically became part of Charlie's routine. If a Japanese tourist tried to take his picture, Charlie would run over, politely borrow the camera, and then imitate the Japanese guy and take *his* picture.

I studied the way Charlie worked the "room" even when there were no walls or ceilings to define it. Regardless of how rowdy they got, Charlie was always in complete control and had a one-liner for every variation of human being in his radius. "What do you call a black Jew? A He-bro . . . What do you call a gay Jew? A He-blew!" Charlie showed us that you can't afford to be subtle when you're working a New York crowd—especially when you don't have a stage or a microphone.

The loud laughs Charlie got reverberated through the park's giant arch and down into the streets and subways. Afterward, Charlie would pass his hat around and collect substantial amounts of money, phone numbers, and drugs. Everybody loved Charlie.

One night he told us the story of how he got hired by *Saturday Night Live*—only to get quickly fired when they figured out he couldn't read. His spot went to Eddie Murphy and the rest is history.

Now, Charlie was the king of the park and that suited him just fine. Over time he became a sort of street mentor to Dave and me. One night as it got dark in the park, rumors starting swirling around that race riots might break out as they had done in Los Angeles the night before in a response to the Rodney King beating. I must admit I was a little jumpy and Charlie offered to walk me home, declaring to everybody in the fountain that tonight it was "every Negro's duty to walk his white friends home safely!"

One sunny afternoon as a crowd was forming, Charlie leaned over and asked Dave and me if we wanted him to introduce us at the end of his show so that we could each jump up and tell a few jokes. He wanted us to feel the rush of a street performance. I was way too scared that my big mouth would get me stabbed. However, my slightly younger and much crazier friend Dave had no fear.

Dave jumped up on a pillar and, emulating Charlie's style, yelled loudly enough to keep the crowd's attention. Charlie sat close by and whispered pointers to Dave. "Talk slower . . . move around . . . watch out for the homeless guy with the shopping cart coming up behind you. . . ."

But eventually, Dave just lit up a cigarette and started speaking in his usual soft manner. He didn't seem to care if folks stopped to listen or just kept walking. Somehow Dave made the crowd of pedestrians and misfits come to his level, like Moses leading his followers through a Red Sea of jokes. Dave seems to work best when he simply gets in front of people, thinks about stuff, and then says those thoughts out loud.

Dave and I became very close to Charlie Barnett before the hard drugs led him to AIDS and a slow, sad demise. Dave continued to honor him by performing in that fountain every weekend for another year or so. This is also when I saw Dave really start to flourish as a comedian. He was no longer performing in his mentor's shadow, and his shows got longer and more complete. Dave had somehow lifted the outdoor comedy mantle from Charlie's shoulders. I believe Dave found his voice in that fountain.

Dave quickly developed into a headliner and was even booked to do stand-up on *Late Show with David Letterman*. Taped at the Ed Sullivan Theater, right smack in the middle of Broadway, this is the definitive credit for any city act. My cousin Tracy and I took Dave to the menswear department at Barney's to buy a suit for his big appearance. Dave, in turn, recommended me for a spot on the *Late Show* as well. My appearance went so well that it became a turning point in my life. Soon afterward I too was headlining around the country.

Of course, Dave eventually became too famous for the park and his impromptu performances would get shut down by the rangers—but I'll always remember our time there as an influential step in our growth as comics and people. And I have no doubt that it was all those extra daylight hours in front of tough outdoor crowds that helped make that skinny kid from D.C. into the comedy heavyweight he is now. Sometimes I wish I'd had the balls to perform in that magical fountain, too. After all, an aspiring Roastmaster needs all the practice he can get.

Not long ago, Dave and I sat in a coffee shop in Las Vegas,

talking about the old days until five in the morning. Since there was a comedy festival happening in town, there were a lot of stand-ups hanging around the lobby. Eventually a young comic from Boston came over to pay his respects and request a photo with Dave and me. When Dave casually asked the guy how everything was going back in Boston, the guy sounded dejected and mentioned that he was having a rough time of it. Dave put his arm around the guy and said, "Don't worry, brother, be patient. You only start out once."

In the flash of that guy's camera, my life had come full circle. That witty whiz kid I'd watched tell jokes in a fountain was suddenly a living legend doling out advice to the rookies.

I still keep an apartment in Greenwich Village and can't walk through Washington Square Park without thinking of those happy days when I too was just starting out.

A ROASTMASTER
MUST SHOW RESPECT

ROASTING IS AN ART, AND the Friars Club is its greatest gallery. Behind its hallowed doors, filthy and disgusting celebrity roasts have been taking place for more than one hundred years. Located in an elegant six-story town house on East Fifty-fifth Street in Manhattan, the Friars is a private, members-only club that caters mainly to people in show business—and Freddie Roman. Since 1904, the Friars has remained a great place to get a brisket sandwich, shoot some pool, take a steam, or just trade zingers with other comedians. The road can be lonely, so it's nice to have the Friars Club to come home to.

Before I became a member, I was invited there a few times as a guest to play poker with some other young stand-ups. I considered it a rare treat because we could play with fancy clay chips while a waiter brought us delicious food and cocktails. I was so used to playing in my friends' tiny overheated apartments that being able to stretch out in the George Burns Card Room on the third floor of the Friars Club was like a three-hour vacation. Plus, in the eve-

MILTON BERLE AND I MOMENTS BEFORE MY FIRST ROAST.

nings, the Friars maintain a "jackets required" dress code, so it was a rare opportunity to break out my bitchin' blue Burberry blazer.

One night on my way up to the poker game, I got to meet one of the greatest comics of all time. The elevator stopped on the second floor and in waddled the great Buddy Hackett. "Hi-ya, fellas," he said out of the corner of his mouth to whomever else happened to be crammed into the elevator. Figuring this was a once-in-a-lifetime chance to meet one of my idols and my parents' all-time favorite comedian, I extended my hand and said, "Mr. Hackett, I don't want to bother you, but I just want to say that I'm a big fan and it's a great honor to meet you." Buddy shook my hand, looked me in the eye, and said, "You know who hates farts the most? Midgets! Because they live at ass height!"

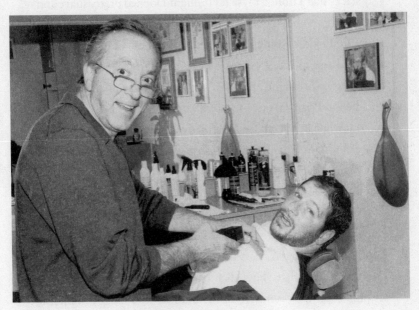

**GETTING A PREROAST SHAVE BY
THE FRIARS' FOLLICLE ARTISTE LUIGI NAPOLITANO.**

Then he slid out of the elevator doors and disappeared. I thought to myself, *Wow, Buddy Hackett just laid a fart joke on me.*

That night as we cashed in our chips, a younger Friar named Greg Fitzsimmons asked me if I would be willing to perform stand-up at a club-sponsored charity golf tournament in honor of his late dad, Bob, who had been a well-known and respected New York radio guy. I jumped at the chance. I perform at charity gigs all the time, but the idea of honoring my friend's dad while sharing a stage with some genuine Catskills comedy legends would be a new adventure—and I love new adventures.

The crowd at the event was mostly comprised of drunken older Friars, who had been playing golf all day at a country club outside the city. I was wearing my blue blazer and a pair of dark gray slacks that I ironed myself. I thought I looked pretty suave and just country clubby enough to fit in. When the Dean of the Friars Club, Freddie Roman, finally introduced me in his trademark loud and pronounced delivery, he said, "Our next comic owns two suits and tonight he is wearing both of them!" Big laughs. Freddie is a Friars favorite and this was definitely his crowd.

But when I got onstage I instinctively fired back. "Jeez, I guess they call him Freddie Roman because you can hear him in fuckin' Italy." More big laughs. So I kept going . . . "Freddie Roman is so loud he can bomb in two comedy clubs at the same time."

Next I went after the other comics on the show. "Wow, what a lineup we got tonight . . . Freddie Roman, Stewie Stone, Dick Capri . . . undertakers, start your engines!"

It was after that show that I began to understand the Friars philosophy, "We only roast the ones we love." I got immense pleasure from the fact that I was able to both honor my friend's dad and raise money for charity simply by making fun of other comics.

A few days later I was invited to join the dais at the annual Friars Club roast. Once a year the Friars honor one of their members with a celebrity luncheon and that year it was going to be the popular martial arts movie star Steven Seagal.

I thought, *Me?! On the dais? Isn't that for living legends? I'm living in a one-bedroom apartment.*

When I got the call from Jean-Pierre Trebot, executive director of the Friars, I thought he was putting me on.

"Hmm . . . are you sure you want me? Jeffrey Ross? From the Comedy Cellar?"

"Yes, we're sure."

"But I've never roasted anybody before. What do I have to do?"

"Just do what you did at the golf tournament."

"But that was just off the top of my head!"

"Yeah, well, you better start preparing then. We'll send a car! Au revoir!"

My mind raced. . . . What had I gotten myself into? How can I possibly make fun of somebody I don't know to his face? How far can you go at these things? Can I curse? Do I have to curse? What if Steven Seagal gets mad and kills me? Or worse yet, makes me watch one of his films?

Obviously, I had a lot of questions. Since this was pre-Google, I went uptown to the Museum of Broadcasting to do some research. I watched some old tapes from the 1970s of Dean Martin in a tux making fun of such obscure friends as John Wayne, Ronald Reagan, Bob Hope, Don Rickles, Lucille Ball, Muhammad

Ali, Jimmy Stewart, Jackie Gleason, Sammy Davis Jr., and Frank Sinatra. That helped me understand the basic gist. It looked like a lot of fun and it was obvious nobody's feelings got hurt.

The only problem was I didn't give two shits about Steven Seagal. But I must admit that the very idea of being able to say whatever I wanted about him right to his face in front of a packed house sounded nothing short of exhilarating. Not to mention the fact that I'd be surrounded by some of comedy's greatest headliners.

I had three weeks to prepare. I started writing insults. Lots of 'em. I tried them out on anybody who would listen. I even went out and bought myself a new suit. After all, I'd be up there with Mr. Television himself, Milton Berle, who would be serving as Roastmaster.

I was very excited to meet Uncle Miltie. Not only had he hosted countless Friars Club roasts but he was considered a national treasure. After breaking into the business as a child actor in Charlie Chaplin's silent films, Milton Berle eventually became a huge star in vaudeville. Then during the early days of television he hosted an immensely popular live sketch comedy show called *The Texaco Star Theater,* and became the biggest star in America. Back then, people actually went out and bought TVs for the first time just so they could watch a grown man run around in a dress on Tuesday nights.

Around the Friars Club, Milton was perhaps best known for something else entirely—the size of his penis. Legend has it that Milton's "joint," as he called it, was the biggest in the biz. Whenever somebody questioned this fact Milton would jokingly challenge that person to a size contest, often threatening to "take out just enough to win." I even heard a story that Milton gave the Friars Club its exquisite thirty-room headquarters as a gift because his new wife decided it was too small for her, Milton, and Milton's penis all to live in together comfortably.

The day of the roast I got up early and whittled down the material I'd written into what I thought was the best ten minutes. Then I read it to my sister over the phone. Then I drank four cups of coffee, put on my new suit, and hopped into the car they sent for me.

The actual Friars "monastery" was also too small to accommodate the crowd for Seagal's roast, so they rented out the Grand Ballroom at the New York Hilton. Backstage there were tons of reporters interviewing people like Donald Trump and Larry King, as well as the guest of honor. It was an exciting scene: comics mingling with politicians . . . Broadway stars mingling with newscasters . . . me fiddling with my material.

Eventually, Monsieur Trebot assembled the roasters in a private room. I got to shake Steven Seagal's hand quickly before we were all led through the kitchen à la *Goodfellas* and out into the brightly lit ballroom stuffed with more than a thousand Friars and their friends. The atmosphere was smoky and boisterous. Every seat was facing the roaster's podium. I had goose bumps. I felt like I'd just walked into my Yankee Stadium.

Because I was the new kid on the dais, Milton didn't put me on until late in the line-up after such legends as Henny Youngman and Buddy Hackett all took turns bashing Seagal, whose movie *Under Siege 2: Dark Territory* had just been released like nerve gas into five thousand theaters around the country.

I didn't actually meet Roastmaster Milton Berle until the moment he brought me up with the most dismissive intro possible, "Our next comedian recently performed at a benefit for lesbians with dildo rash . . . Jeffrey Ross!"

I strode up to the podium with as much confidence as I could fake. I shook Steven Seagal's hand, looked out at a sea of strangers staring back at me, and calmly said, "I realize a lot of you don't know me, but I feel uniquely qualified to be here today 'cause I'm also a shitty actor."

Everybody laughed. I felt like I had hit a homer off my first pitch. I continued. "Seriously, Mr. Seagal, I went to see your new movie *Under Siege 2* . . . but it was so bad I walked out during the previews. Honestly, folks, what can you really say about Steven Seagal that hasn't already been said about Jean-Claude Van Damme? . . . Is he laughing? Is he laughing?" Thankfully, he was. Well, he was at least smiling. Probably fake smiling. But at least he wasn't hitting me in the face with a roundhouse kick.

I was on a roll. And for some reason this made Milton Berle crazy. Every time I got a big laugh, he jabbed his long, pointy index finger right into my ribs. Of course, nobody else could see this because I was behind a podium and he was sitting right beside me. The audience must've thought I had some weird shtick-tic.

After a few minutes I couldn't take it anymore. This crazy old fuck was blowing my flow. I finally turned to Milton and said, "By the way, folks, you never know what you're gonna see in New York . . . I was walking around downtown this morning and I saw Milton Berle in an antique shop . . . eight hundred bucks." Milton jumped up and leered at me, pretending to be offended.

The crowd was eating it up so I took a couple more shots. "Folks, Milton Berle is so old he's his own influence. I'm tellin' ya, most of his jokes were stolen off of cave walls." But nothing could stop him. Milton kept interrupting me and poking me in the ribs and stealing the crowd's attention. I was getting flustered. I was losing control. Finally, Buddy Hackett yelled from his seat, "Hey, Milton! Let the kid work! Don't you remember when you used to?" The crowd erupted in applause. Not one to be upstaged, Milton ran down the dais and planted a big wet kiss on Buddy's mouth. This resulted in even bigger applause and cheering.

Then in an attempt to regain control I said, "Well, there you have it, folks . . . Milton Berle and Buddy Hackett—between the two of 'em there's over a hundred and fifty years of homosexual experience!" The crowd went bananas as Milton ran back over and kissed me on the cheek. I sat back down to a standing ovation. There is no tougher crowd than the Friars—and I had just killed 'em.

I remember wishing my parents had been around to see it. They would've gotten a real kick out of watching me up there riffing with comedy's kings.

Afterward, it's Friars tradition for the roasters to go back to the club to have a drink (Hackett) or a cigar (Berle) and brag about their performances. But that day all anybody could talk about was the new kid on the dais.

Over a whiskey, I asked Buddy Hackett what made him come to my rescue earlier. He told me that Milton Berle got jealous when other comics got more laughs than him, and that when he saw me flinching he knew Milton was probably poking me in the ribs. "He's been doing that to young comics for years. That means you're funny," Buddy said.

Buddy's pep talk gave me the confidence to go over and talk to Milton. I asked him for some tips for my next roast. He told me to do less time and tell fewer jokes. "They only remember the home runs, kid." Great roast wisdom that I still use today.

Then he shoved the end of a cigar into his right nostril and inhaled deeply. He claimed Fidel Castro sent him cigars for Hanukkah and said that if it doesn't smell like horseshit, it wasn't a genuine Cuban. Then he stuck it in my mouth and handed me a lit match as if passing me a torch.

What a day. What a dais. Who would have imagined that my first roast would be Milton Berle's last?

Milton spent his last couple of years in a wheelchair hanging around the other Friars Club in Beverly Hills. We became rather friendly during that time, often sharing a sandwich and a cigar. He told lots of great stories and was always very sweet to me and other young comics.

Even though he was old and frail, his mind was still sharp and his "joint" was still gigantic. I only know this because he showed it off to me. (I know this sounds weird, but hey, it's showbiz, baby!) He had just finished his chopped liver on rye when he asked me to help him walk over to the men's room. When we got to the urinal he unzipped his trousers and turned toward me ever so slightly, allowing me a brief glimpse. I couldn't help but take a peek. I thought an anaconda had escaped from the zoo. All Milton said was, "Believe the hype."

The last time I saw Milton he was in the audience when I performed at Sid Caesar's seventy-fifth birthday party. I said, "Look, everybody, the great Uncle Miltie is here tonight—and he brought a wheelchair for his cock." Milton loved the attention. He somehow managed to leap to his feet and yell, "My cock is fine! This wheelchair is for my balls!"

Ironically, Milton's funeral wound up being a sort of Roast-master's graduation for me. The service was funny, emotional, and star-studded. As everybody filed out of the chapel and headed toward the burial site, I slipped into one of the family waiting rooms to pee. I couldn't have been in there more than forty-five seconds. When I opened the door I found none other than Roast-master extraordinaire Don Rickles standing there with his hands on his hips looking as if he'd been waiting for hours. He looked me up and down and said, "What took so long? Was there a dais in there?"

Wowie! I thought as I zipped up my fly. *Rickles knows who I am! And not only that—he just made fun of me for doing the roasts!* Suddenly I felt like I was on the roasting map. Uncle Miltie would be proud. I really miss that crazy old man. Long Live the Roast-master!

THE SHTICK-UP ARTIST: THE ROASTMASTER'S GUIDE TO ROMANCE

I'VE NEVER MET A TRUE Roastmaster who isn't adept at picking up members of the opposite sex. In the case of Andy Dick, I'm not even sure what the opposite sex is. But the point is, being a Roastmaster just seems to make you more fuckable. Research shows that when one human being watches another human being who is insulting a bunch of other human beings, certain chemicals are released in the brain that trigger a sexual response. Put simply, women are attracted to bad boys—especially funny ones.

Look at me. I think we can all agree that if I weren't a comedian I'd be dating a girl who looks like Gilbert Gottfried with long hair. Instead, I have a stunning girlfriend named Megan, who makes a mean Texas bean dip and laughs at all my jokes. She comes to every single one of my shows. Watching me kill turns her on.

Even she can't seem to explain why—it just does. "If you can make me laugh—you can make me do anything," she told me as I changed tapes in the video camera.

In prehistoric times, I'd have to impress a woman by slaying a saber-toothed tiger instead of a bucktoothed heckler. Scientists tell us that women have been programmed by evolution to be attracted to men who can dominate other men. Thankfully, you don't have to cut off a woolly mammoth's dick and beat your fellow tribesmen over the head with it. We're lucky enough to live in an advanced civilization that appreciates and re-wards wit. As Roastmasters, we just have to bust a few balls and sooner or later, we're busting a nut back at the crib.

Now it's your turn. As your roasting skills im-prove, you'll probably want to embark on a night of carousing to see if you can roast your way into someone's pants. Here is a simple three-step exer-cise for hopeless Roastmantics looking to find that special someone.

1. MARK YOUR TERRITORY

Immediately let everyone know who's in charge. Cats, monkeys, and dogs do this through urina-tion. Roastmasters do it through vilification. In other words, you'll be dissing instead of pissing. So make fun of the overweight bartender. Lampoon the hairy waitress. Just don't piss off the steroidal bouncer. It's virtually impossible to pick up a chick when you're unconscious AND ugly.

2. LOCATE A POTENTIAL ROASTMISTRESS

Now that you've insulted everyone in your radius, the women should be warmed up. Whichever lookers are laughing the hardest, those are your primary targets. When telling a joke to a group of people, look in a pretty woman's eyes right as you say the punch line. This way, you two will share the laugh together. It will be your first romantic moment. As soon as the opportunity arises, you should try teasing her gently about her appearance. If she can't take a joke, don't take her home. Below are some sample pickup putdowns:

What happened? Nose job didn't take?

Didn't I see you on *Bulgaria's Next Top Model*?

Seriously, you're really a fashion model? For what, maternity clothes?

You have gorgeous eyebrows. They really go with your sideburns.

Tell me, are you a natural two-tone? Because you've got blacker roots than Kunta Kinte.

You have such a pronounced nose. Was your father a pelican?

Nice blouse, is it reversible? No? Then is it returnable?

A pretty girl like you should think about getting her teeth fixed.

Normally I don't like it when one boob is so much bigger than the other, but it seems to work on you.

Sure, any shlub can shower a shorty with flattery, but only a true Roastmaster can get a woman to laugh at herself. Once a woman thinks you're funny, your finger practically smells already.

3. SAY SOMETHING NICE

Just like at a roast, you should try to close the deal by putting on a serious face and saying something sweet. For example, "You seem really interesting and kind." "It takes a special type of soul to care about homeless cats." "I'm sure your grandmother really appreciated you being with her at the end." This will touch her heart and pretty soon she'll be touching that podium in your pants.

But remember, finding true love is never easy. A Roastmaster's Roastmistress must understand what the very wise Buddy Hackett once referred to as the "artistic temperament." That's right, we Roastmasters are moody. Sometimes we are even complete assholes. Some would say our charm is our lack of charm. And if it happens to be a night we don't have a show, we'll instinctively start making fun of whoever is around. Therefore, our women must be of a very rare mold. Not only must they be ego-boosting and eternally optimistic, they must also have the patience of a saint and skin thicker than a triceratops's.

I once had a girlfriend who never laughed at my jokes. I called her my unamused muse, which is probably why it didn't last. It's

I ONCE ASKED BUDDY WHAT THE SECRET TO A LONG MARRIAGE WAS. HE SAID, "EVERY MORNING I GET UP, WALK OVER TO MY WIFE'S SIDE OF THE BED, AND SAY, 'MY DARLING, HAVE I DONE ANYTHING TO UPSET YOU YET TODAY?' "

important for a Roastmaster to be surrounded by positive energy, good vibes, and big tits. Then who knows what might happen? One day you may even find the girl of your dreams, settle down, and pop out a few Roastmunchkins. With any luck, they'll inherit your superior funny bone and not your inferior bone structure, you poor misshapen bastard.

A ROASTMASTER
MUST ENJOY THE PROCESS

*A*S THE NEW MILLENNIUM APPROACHED, I was living in Greenwich Village and doing stand-up every single night. Much of my family was still in nearby Jersey and my beloved Friars Club was only a cab ride away. I had earned tenure and respect in all of the city's comedy clubs and could roll onstage whenever I wanted to try out new material. I'd usually open with a joke about New York: "You guys really cheered me up . . . I wrecked my car today . . . I hit a deer . . . Thirty-fourth and Broadway . . . How the hell does that happen? Poor thing ran out of Penn Station with a hot pretzel hanging out of its mouth. Then a homeless guy ran out of nowhere and squeegied the deer right off my windshield. I bet you the deer and the squeegee guy were working together. I'm tellin' ya, everything's a scam in this fucking city."

I was truly enjoying my life as full-time comedian and part-time roaster. Over time I'd learned not to get too stressed out about bad auditions or cranky club owners. Since I had never planned a life in show business in the first place, I figured that simply telling jokes that I wrote myself in front of an audience was more than I could ever want out of life. Between my addictions to the chicken salad at Bagel Bob's on University Place and the waitresses at the Comedy Cellar on MacDougal Street, I thought nothing could drag me from my comedy wonderland.

But then one day radio guys Jimmy Kimmel and Adam Carolla called from Los Angeles and asked me to help them start up a new TV project called *The Man Show*. My job, if I chose to accept it, would be to help them come up with material about stuff guys enjoy such as basketball, booze, and boobs. In fact, Jimmy told me every episode would end with a slow-motion montage of beautiful women jumping on trampolines. That's when I decided a steady paycheck was just what the Roastmaster needed.

ADAM, ME, AND JIMMY ON A BEER RUN. GOOD TIMES!

I froze my account at the Friars, locked up my one-bedroom cave, and headed west in search of bicoastiality. After an exhaustive search that included a depressing array of guesthouses, pool houses, halfway houses, and outhouses, I finally found a sun-drenched studio on the ninth floor of an eleven-story high-rise with a pool, a gym, indoor parking, and lots of hot chicks. Like a scene from *Bugsy*, I told Sylvia, the real estate agent, "I don't care what it costs—I'll take it!"

Sylvia said, "There is one other thing that I must disclose as required by law."

"Shoot, Sylvia," I shouted as I admired the breathtaking view.

She said, "You should know that the last person to live in this apartment committed suicide."

"Really?" I said. "Did you know him?"

"Yeah. Sweet guy. About your age. He was a writer."

I quickly scanned the place. "Where did he do it?" I asked. She pointed to the balcony and motioned that he jumped. I instinctively backed away from the railing, thanked Sylvia for her time, and headed for the elevator faster than you can say *Geronimo!*

After another couple of weeks of sleeping on my friend's pull-out couch, Sylvia called back with a new listing in the same building that she claimed had the best unobstructed view of Hollywood she'd ever seen. I quickly finished typing up a *Man Show* sketch about a new line of *wife leashes,* and went to look for myself.

Sylvia wasn't shittin' me. From the balcony of apartment 9C, I could see all the way from the skyscrapers in downtown Los Angeles to the billboards on the Sunset Strip and up to the mansions in the Hollywood Hills. However, if I turned my head too far to the right I would be in full view of apartment 9A, where that poor depressed writer about my age once jumped off the balcony.

I leaned over and looked down. I wasn't sure if I could handle the constant reminder of how tough this business can be. After sitting out there for ten minutes, I decided not to let it bother me. Still, before committing to a long-term lease, I asked my manager Barry to come by for a second opinion. He wasn't in the door three seconds when he looked straight out at the view and said, "This place is unbelievable, man!" I gave Sylvia a hug and the deposit right there on the balcony.

My move-in date happened to be Oscars night. As I stood on my new balcony and watched those klieg lights bounce around the sky, both my heart and schmeckel danced with anticipation as I pondered the opportunities this new town might bring me. As the limos clogged the streets below, I fantasized that perhaps one day I too might attend Hollywood's most glamorous affair.

In the meantime, I had to settle for good times at *The Man Show* and weekend lunches at the *other* Friars Club, in Beverly Hills. Although this West Coast branch wasn't nearly as populated or sophisticated as the club in New York, it did allow me an occasional shvitz, kibbitz, or nosh with such legendary roastmasters as Red Buttons, Milton Berle, and Sid Caesar. At Sid's seventy-fifth birthday party, I goofed on the fact that everybody in the club was even older than he was. "Sid, have you noticed there's no kids allowed in the club but yet there's still a diaper-changing station in the men's room?"

I also started making friends with people in my apartment building. I'll never forgive Michelle the publicist from the sixth floor, who once invited me to a restaurant opening where I got explosive diarrhea. Residing up in the penthouse was Ken the producer, who told me Buddy Hackett once chased him around a postproduction facility with a butcher knife because he didn't like

SHARING A SMOKE AND A LAUGH WITH MILTON BERLE, RED BUTTONS, AND SID CAESAR—THREE LEGENDS WHOSE HEADS SHOULD BE CARVED INTO MOUNT ROASTMORE.

the way he had edited his HBO comedy special (a story Buddy later confirmed). And of course, there was Angelique the hooker from the third floor, who flashed me her boobs for a cup of my Clorox in the laundry room late one night. There were a lot of quirky people around and I was starting to feel right at home.

One afternoon while I was writing a *Man Show* sketch about a new line of Whoopi Goldberg whoopee cushions with which *you* are supposed to fart on *her,* I suddenly heard loud techno music, looked up from my laptop, and saw that somebody had finally moved into that creepy apartment across from mine. It was another guy *about my age.* He was naked. And he was dancing. He saw me just as I saw him. He waved and I waved back. Then he went back to dancing all by himself. "Welcome to Hollywood," I mumbled as I went back to my ridiculous sketch.

The next day my new neighbor and I ran into each other in the elevator and he apologized for the loud music and the full frontal nudity. He told me his name was Rob and that he was an actor—which wasn't surprising because he was dressed as a waiter. I asked him if he was bothered by the fate of the former tenant of his apartment and he told me he was . . . until they knocked a chunk of money off the rent and now he rarely thought about it. "With a view like ours, it's easy to forget such unpleasantries," he said as we shook hands and headed off to our separate lives.

When I wasn't at *The Man Show* studios being put in a head-lock by Jimmy Kimmel's cousin Sal or throwing the medicine ball around the gym at the Beverly Hills Friars Club, I was usually hanging out on my sunny balcony.

At night, I'd sit out there with friends and smoke cigars and whatever else and stare at the stars in the sky. As a tribute to my past life in New York I bought a print of a painting by John Lennon in which he depicts himself as the Statue of Liberty, and hung it over my leopard-skin couch. I even bought some candles and a

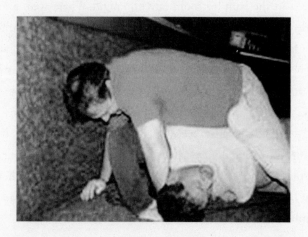

fancy bench from Thailand in an attempt to make my three-by-nine ledge into Jew Jeffner's mini–Playboy Mansion.

I adapted to L.A. with shocking alacrity. I started drinking overcaffeinated lattes and getting overpriced haircuts at the same salon as Arnold Schwarzenegger. I was becoming that stereotypical Hollywood douche I'd laughed at in Woody Allen movies. I even bought myself a Porsche convertible to complete the total prick package. Still, it was better than emceeing for sixty bucks a show at the Bennigan's in Plainfield, New Jersey.

By the end of that year, *The Man Show* was officially picked up for a second season. Although it was the most fun job I ever had, I pulled myself away in search of new adventures. I started to see Hollywood as a magical place where unbelievable things were happening to me. . . .

One week I was poisoned and killed by my opening act on a particularly gruesome episode of *CSI*. Another week, I beat out a thousand "guys my age" to costar with Valerie Harper in a prime-time sitcom pilot. I also learned to punch up movie scripts with the very funny Farrelly brothers. I even performed on a bunch of West Coast roasts with such killer comics as Norm Crosby, Jack Carter, Dom Irrera, and Bill Maher.

On one very special occasion, I was asked to perform my stand-up act at a West Coast Friars Club charity event honoring Don Rickles. Being asked to entertain the world's greatest living insult comic and his family was a moment I'll always cherish. I don't remember too many of the jokes I said that night but I do recall knocking him out with one of my signature love poems. . . .

The orchestra started tinkling underneath me as I asked for the lights to be dimmed and said, "This is a poem that my dad wrote for my mom. It's called 'Enough with the Bread Already.' 'Your smile blooms like a bright summer flower . . . Your hair flows down like a soft rain shower . . . Your eyes are like open seas, blue from coast to coast . . . So how come your ass looks like a truck? Enough with the bread already!' "

Anyway, I must've been funny that night because a short time later I got this note from Mr. Warmth himself.

DON RICKLES

September 12, 2000

Dear Jeff,

Just a note to thank you for being at my Friar's event. You are certainly a bright and a new talented guy. As you could tell, my family and I, and certainly the audience enjoyed you immensely.

Wishing you great success. Thanks again.

As ever,

Don

Getting this sort of validation from the Sultan of Insulting was just the boost I needed to fully embrace my own ball-busting persona.

Indeed, it was a fun time to be me. I even did a roast for wheelchair-bound *Hustler* publisher Larry Flynt, in which I called him, among other things, Humpty Pussy. Who says you can't roast the handicapped? It was a fun night and afterward I got asked out by a sexy actress who works in pornos. I said, "Okay, what night do you want to go out?" She said, "Well, I'm working Tuesday and Wednesday. How about Thursday?" I made a face and said, "How about Monday?"

My life was just one decadent experience after another. I regularly puffed illegal Cohibas with Uncle Miltie at the Friars Club and mind-bending spliffs with strippers and rappers at parties in the Hollywood Hills. I even got myself invited to the next Academy Awards.

A few years earlier, I had written Billy Crystal a fan letter telling him that if he ever hosted the Academy Awards again I wanted to help write jokes. I included the unedited footage from my first Comedy Central roast in which I drop killers like "Drew Carey is to comedy what Mariah Carey is to comedy." Lo and behold, almost two years later my manager got a call.

When I first walked into Mr. Saturday Night's spacious office I figured I was there for some intense interview or to take some comedy quiz to test my improv skills. However, before I even sat down, the gold standard of Oscar hosts shook my trembling hand and asked me to join his elite writing team. He told me it would be a two-and-a-half-month commitment and that I was expected to write jokes on my own so he could read them aloud at the weekly brainstorming sessions. I was elated and accepted his offer on the spot.

I planted myself on the balcony, booted up my laptop, and tried to mine humor from such depressing movies as *Boys Don't Cry, The Green Mile, American Beauty, The Cider House Rules,* and *The Sixth Sense,* with that gloomy catchphrase, "I see dead people." The first joke I wrote down summed up my predicament. "This year's best films deal with ghosts, prison life, the tobacco industry, abortion, and statutory rape—and that was just in *Deuce Bigalow: Male Gigolo.*"

I sat there for hours alone in the dark trying to think up jokes about *The Sixth Sense*'s adorable young star Haley Joel Osment, such as this one—"Hey, kid, nice tux . . . you borrow it from Al Pacino?"—when suddenly I spotted my neighbor Rob once again dancing in the buff.

It's not that I was spying on him, it's just that our balconies faced each other and his little pink ass was right there in plain view. "I see naked people," I mumbled to myself as I ducked inside and went to bed thinking of anything else.

He and I hardly spoke to each other, but we definitely knew a lot about each other. He could always see what was happening in my life and I could always see what *was not* happening in his. Whether he was dancing naked to "It's Raining Men" or just smoking cigarettes on his balcony, Rob always seemed to be all alone.

Before I knew it, the big night of the Academy Awards arrived. I'd been in town exactly a year and already my first-night fantasy had come true: I was heading to Tinseltown's most prestigious event. As I left in my tuxedo, I spotted Rob sitting on his balcony alone. I waved but I'm pretty sure he pretended not to see me.

That night, Billy Crystal absolutely killed in front of millions of people. Watching such an incredibly skilled showman perform material we had worked on together was truly one of the most exciting experiences of my life. Although I contributed a bunch of great jokes to the opening monologue and musical number, it is Roastmaster tradition never to reveal which ones exactly.

I also got to stand backstage during the live show and pitch jokes on the fly. From the wings, we spotted Best Actress nominee Annette Bening in the very front row holding her very pregnant belly. I tried a few lines out on Billy: "Annette is so pregnant, if she wins, the baby is liable to reach out and grab the statue"? Billy laughed but the show's producers looked at me like they were about to call security. "Annette, if you're gonna have a baby, can you at least wait until after my musical number? Births are hard to follow!" I honestly can't remember which jokes he wound up telling on the show and which ones just made us laugh at rehearsal. Either way, I had learned more working with Billy for two months than I had in the previous ten years I'd been doing comedy.

Halfway through the show I spotted Arnold Schwarzenegger pacing in the wings. He was about to present the Oscar for Best Foreign Film and was quietly practicing his lines. I looked down and noticed his pant leg was stuck in the top of his cowboy boot. "Excuse me, Mr. Schwarzenegger?" "Yah?" he said, without looking up from his script. "I'm sorry to bother you, but I thought you'd want to fix your pants before you go out there." He looked down and yelled, "Oh fuck! Thank you so much! Maria forgot to check me over before I left my chair." He must have known I

ME AND MY IDOL BILLY CRYSTAL WHO HAS TEMPORARILY
TRANSFORMED INTO HIS IDOL SAMMY DAVIS JR.
FOR AN OSCARS OPENING FILM PIECE I HELPED WRITE.

was one of the writers because he added, "Please tell Billy great show."

What a thrill. What an honor. What a gift basket. Writing an Academy Awards opening with Billy Crystal and his team was like playing for the Yankees of comedy. Afterward, we all went to the Governor's Ball where I got drunk and soaked in the audience's accolades and Billy's appreciation. When I got home, I walked out on the balcony to smoke a cigar with the smokin' redhead who did Billy's makeup, and not surprisingly, there was my neighbor Rob still sitting alone on his balcony. We just ignored each other as usual. The next day, I locked up my apartment and headed out on the road for a week of stand-up performances, feeling exhausted and confident.

When I got back to my apartment the following week, I stopped at the front desk to pick up my mail. Although it was a sunny Sunday, the usually chipper security guards seemed down. I went to see who was hanging out by the pool, but there was nobody. In fact, even the laundry room and the gym seemed to be deserted. I went upstairs and sat on my balcony. I looked down and no one was playing tennis either.

This eerie feeling went on for another day before I finally went down to the lobby and asked the head of security, Captain Beard, why the place was such a ghost town.

He looked at me curiously. "You mean, you don't know about your neighbor . . . ?"

"The old lady in 9B? Is she okay?" I asked.

"No, on the other side—the waiter in 9A."

"The actor—Rob? What happened?"

Captain Beard whispered, "He's dead."

"Dead?!"

"Yup. Fell off his balcony."

"What?! Really? When?"

"Day before yesterday."

I was speechless for almost a minute. Finally, I said, "That's the same apartment as the last guy who jumped?" Captain Beard just nodded.

"It must've been awful."

"He put on quite a show."

"What do you mean?"

"It was eight o'clock in the morning . . . Kids getting ready for school. The whole building saw it from their balconies. It was terrible. He just climbed over the side of the railing and started screaming, not making any sense. People tried to talk him down but he wouldn't listen. Just kept saying that somebody was chasing him. Everybody figures he must've been on drugs."

"Was he naked?"

Captain Beard nodded.

"He was always fucking naked. Captain Beard, I'm sorry you had to go through this again. I can't imagine—"

"You don't want to imagine."

"I don't think I want to know any more. Thanks, Captain. Hang in there."

My lonely, out-of-work, naked, gay, actor neighbor was dead. I felt sad that he was gone, but also slightly relieved that I had missed the entire gory affair. I stopped going out on the balcony. In fact, none of the other tenants seemed to be using theirs either. Clearly nobody wanted to be reminded of that awful morning. I tried to put it out of my mind, too. Still, I couldn't help but wonder why two tenants in a row jumped out of apartment 9A.

The next day, I tried to put the incident out of my mind as I made my way to the Beverly Hills Friars Club for an afternoon roasting of New York Yankees manager Joe Torre. As I sat there on the dais between Billy Crystal and Milton Berle, about to make fun of one of my biggest sports idols to his face, I felt like I was finally becoming a made man in the comedy world. The beloved player-turned-coach was seated between his brother Frank Torre and his good pal from the West Coast Tommy Lasorda. I felt invincible that day and opened strong with a fastball down the middle. "Wow, I haven't seen this many Italians behind a microphone since the Valachi hearings." Then I tagged it up with a curveball. "But seriously, who knows more about baseball bats than the Italian people?" As usual, Uncle Miltie tried to interrupt me. But I was fully prepared with comebacks . . .

"Milton Berle is such a big baseball fan that on opening day he threw out his balls."

"Milton Berle's dick is so big it's got a warning track."

"I hear Milton's dick is so big he jerks off with pine tar."

"They should send that cock to Cooperstown!"

Of course, Joe Torre didn't know who the hell I was, but he still seemed to be enjoying himself—even when I told him that he was living proof that bad players can make great coaches. "I once saw Joe Torre strike out in two pitches!"

The next morning, I woke up with a hangover bigger than Milton Berle's cock. While closing my curtains, I spotted my neighbor Rob's mom crying inside his apartment. I looked down and saw the dented patch of dead grass where his body had landed. Even as I think of it now my eyes well up and my head starts to pound. This poor guy must have been in so much pain inside to do this to himself and his mother.

As I lay in bed that night, I suddenly felt like somebody else besides the blonde sleeping next to me was in the room. I opened my eyes and sat up. I saw nothing, but I felt a presence that stayed with me all night. I just lay there with one eye open, clenching a tennis racket until the sun came up.

The very next night, I was awakened by a faint howl that got louder and louder until it almost sounded like a man screaming in pain. Or perhaps for my attention. I got up and went into the other room to shut the balcony door—only to find that it had been closed the whole time. And over time other weird shit started happening. Twice, I saw small Texas tornadoes suddenly whip up in the courtyard right in between my apartment and

Rob's, sending debris up to our balconies on the ninth floor. I also was shocked to find that a bunch of heavy tiles on my ceiling were inexplicably out of place, exposing the dark, hollow guts of the building.

I continued to feel a strangeness inside my apartment. I decided that my dead neighbor might now be my invisible roommate and I lived with a sickening feeling that Rob was now a tortured soul reaching out for some kind of acknowledgment. Out of fear and respect, I didn't talk about him while I was in the apartment. I didn't want to anger him or cause him more grief. I figured eventually he would figure out that I wasn't his type and go wherever he was supposed to go to next. Of course, my friends thought the whole thing was hilarious. After all, a cynical comic like me is the last guy you'd think would believe in ghosts. Jimmy Kimmel even tried to sneak his uncle Frank into my apartment to scare the shit out of me.

Then one rainy night as I lay in bed I heard a loud BANG from the other room. Then another. I tried to ignore the racket, but it got louder. I ran into the living room and the large framed painting by John Lennon that hung over my couch was somehow lifting itself up and then dropping back down against the wall. I stood there dumbfounded for a minute before running back into my bedroom and closing the door. I just lay there under the covers for hours, scared shitless and alone, trying to decide what to do.

Finally I couldn't take it anymore. I leaped up, wrapped myself in a blanket, walked into the living room, and yanked the balcony door wide open. I stepped outside into the cold air, looked up at the sky over the courtyard, and said, "Why are you scaring me like this?!"

I continued, in a respectful tone, "I'm sorry for what happened to you. I'm sorry for your agony. I'm sorry I wasn't here when it happened. And I'm sorry I didn't get to know you better. I can't imagine what you must have gone through to get to that place. I hope wherever you go from here, that it's better for you. And I won't forget you."

I just stood there another minute. Everything suddenly seemed calm. Then I did something I hadn't done in a while. I lit a cigar. I took a few puffs . . . then I lit a second one and tossed it off the balcony into the wind—"for Rob the Actor," I said.

Sometimes I wonder why Rob chose to haunt me. I thought maybe he resented me, or perhaps just wanted me to appreciate what I had—friends, a career—all the things he missed out on. Maybe all he wanted was for me to acknowledge his pain. His disappointment. His struggle. In a way, I was flattered that he reached out to me. This tortured soul—an actor, giving one last performance.

A short time later I had a big audition for *Saturday Night Live*. Producer Lorne Michaels was attempting to find a new anchor for the coveted "Weekend Update" fake news segment. After a successful screen test it came down to me and the show's talented head writer, Tina Fey. Lorne asked me to fly to New York for one last meeting.

My manager at the time, the legendary Bernie Brillstein, told me it was a great sign that Lorne wanted to see me in person. "Lorne likes to tell people the good news himself," Bernie said. We started getting calls of congratulations from network executives. I even ran into cast member Will Ferrell on the street and he welcomed me aboard.

For a young insult comic, nothing could have been more exciting than a chance to roast the news every week in front of a national audience on such a popular show. I gave my plants away, locked up my haunted apartment, and headed to New York for my exciting face-to-face meeting with Lorne Michaels.

However, when I finally got to his office, Lorne told me that even though my audition was outstanding, he was getting a lot of pressure from his cast to promote from within. He said he'd let me know in the morning. So I went out and got drunk. Sure enough, Lorne woke me up with his epiphany. He was going with up-and-coming Tina Fey and cast member Jimmy Fallon as the coed co-anchors of *Weekend Update*.

Show business can be tough. Sometimes even heartbreaking. But you can't let it crush your spirit. That's why I never let myself get too excited when things are going well, and I never let myself get too sad when things go bad. I try to stay somewhere in the middle. I try to take the good with the bad. I try to relish the bombing as much as the killing. I try to enjoy the process.

When I got back to my apartment I instinctively stepped out onto the balcony to admire the view. Maybe in another life I'll get to thank my pushy poltergeist for what he did. He forced me to slow down and assess how good I had it. I had my health. I was making lots of friends. I was working with my idols. And I was lucky enough to be doing something I loved. Above all, a Roast-master must appreciate what he has, even if it is a fleeting figment of his imagination.

THE ROAST MUST GO ON

*O*CCASIONALLY I GET BACK TO the East Coast to do a gig or visit family. On one particular trip I found myself following the talented and untiring Jamie Foxx around to nightclubs, comedy clubs, and recording studios until 4 a.m. a bunch of nights in a row.

We were in town for the MTV Video Music Awards. He was hosting. I was his head writer. The show, broadcast live from Lincoln Center, was a smash and I even got to watch a nubile Britney Spears writhe around the stage with a twelve-foot python (no, not the one that lives in Jamie Foxx's pants).

Afterward, Jamie took me out all night, got me completely fucked up, and then I crashed for two days straight. I was finally awakened by a cacophony of sirens. At first I thought they were in my dream. But then I heard the voice of my friend Ralphie May yelling at me in his loud Southern rasp, "Ross! Wake up! You there? Pick up the fucking phone!" I finally opened my eyes and realized his voice was coming out of my answering machine. I grabbed the receiver and said groggily, "What, Ralphie?"

"You okay, man?"

"Yeah, I'm fine. Why?"

"Weren't you supposed to fly back to L.A. today?"

"Yeah, later on. . . . What's up?"

"Terrorist attack right in your neighborhood!"

"Huh???" Quickly, I turned on my TV. Sure enough, the shit was going down less than a mile away. A never-ending caravan of emergency vehicles careened by my high-rise apartment at 300 Mercer Street, as I watched the mayhem on TV. I saw people jumping out of windows. Then one by one the towers collapsed. I tried to call friends who lived farther downtown, but my phones were dead.

I quickly pulled on some pants and went into crisis mode. Anticipating downtowners seeking refuge, I ran to a bank machine for some cash and went to the deli and bought a bunch of provisions (mostly chicken salad sandwiches). By the time I returned, ten minutes later, Dave Chappelle and his wife, Elaine, were standing outside my apartment, holding their new baby boy, waiting for me with gray ash all over their clothes and hair. The air began to smell like burning flesh, so we went inside and sat on my couch feeling helpless and scared. Police blocked off the entire neighborhood and didn't allow anybody in or out. Eventually, a few more people showed up seeking temporary refuge. After a while we all just went up to the roof and watched the smoke billow away from what is now known as Ground Zero.

DAVE CHAPPELLE TOOK THIS PICTURE WITH THE WORLD TRADE CENTER SMOLDERING BEHIND ME.

The next day my apartment was empty again and I searched for some way to help. At this point, most of the firemen from my local station house were presumed dead and nobody knew how many civilians were still trapped under the rubble. I inquired about donating blood at the hospital, but they said they had enough. I didn't know what to do with myself. After a few days of watching all the sad news, I began to wonder if I'd ever work again. Was comedy over?

By the end of the week I got a call from Comedy Central. They told me that this year's roast would almost certainly be canceled because of the tragedy. The network reasoned that since the roast was only two and a half weeks away it would be inappropriate to go on with the show.

I hung up with mixed feelings. On one hand, I understood and respected the fact that the towers were still smoldering. But on the other hand, I thought that a couple of laughs in a couple of weeks might be welcome.

As usual, I called Buddy Hackett. I asked him what happened when President Kennedy was assassinated. He told me he was booked in Las Vegas, and although the casino never actually shut down, he did cancel some shows. But then he began to feel bad for the people who had come there for vacation just to see him. He said scores of tourists were walking around the lobby and the pool like depressed zombies. So the night after the televised funeral, he "walked out onstage and said, 'We all lost a president. I lost a president and a friend—and I hope he's on his way to heaven and resting in peace. And that's the last thing I'm going to say about it.' And then I went to work."

That's when it hit me right in my thick but patriotic skull: The roast must go on! This year's scheduled honoree was none other than *Playboy* founder Hugh Hefner, who personifies all the reasons the terrorists hate us in the first place. At the request of Jean-Pierre, the executive director of the Friars, I dashed off a letter to the club's board of governors and the executives at Comedy Central to try to convince them all that if we didn't put on our tuxedos and make jokes about Hef's seven matching blond girlfriends, then the terrorists would win by forfeit. I suggested we scrap the lavish after-party and divert those funds to the families who lost loved ones.

Luckily, everybody agreed, and I began the difficult task of convincing a nervous Sarah Silverman that it was safer than ever to fly. Of course, she didn't believe me, but she manned up and flew in anyway. In fact, so did my other brave friends, Drew Carey, Artie Lange, Rob Schneider, Ice-T, Cedric the Entertainer, Adam Carolla, and Jimmy Kimmel, who served as the evening's Roastmaster. When I first introduced Jimmy to Sarah backstage at rehearsal, there were no romantic sparks that I could detect, but there were certainly some comedic sparks. In fact, her opening line that night was, "Jimmy Kimmel—you're fat and you have no charisma . . . watch your back, Danny Aiello!" Back then, Jimmy was still hosting *The Man Show* and I could see in his face how psyched he was that a hot chick even knew who he was. Whoever could have guessed this moment would launch the greatest dais-inspired love affair since Slappy White hooked up with Moms Mabley?

An eclectic collection of New York luminaries showed up just to watch, including fake news correspondents Steve Carell and Stephen Colbert, egomaniacal developer Donald Trump, menopausal rocker Debbie Harry, rookie sportscaster Rich Eisen, pubescent actor Samm Levine, "artist" LeRoy Neiman, unemployed guitarist Ace Frehley, and former hostage turned inmate Patty Hearst. At the preshow cocktail party I asked her if she was going to be okay with all the cursing. She said, "Oh, please—I've been to fucking prison!"

Still, I sensed a melancholy mood as I entered the gigantic banquet hall, sporting an old-fashioned bow tie given to me by Buddy Hackett. After a brief and effective "Let's try to get back to normal"–themed preamble by the lovable Freddie Roman, Roastmaster Kimmel fearlessly set the tone for the night. "He's been called a visionary, a genius, and pioneer of free speech, but when I think of Hugh Hefner what comes to mind is rubbing my dong until it squirts. He is an inspiration to masturbation. He's the George Washington of jacking off . . ."

Hef, who looked dashing in his tuxedo, was already laughing harder than anybody else in the room. Kimmel was on a roll. "I could go on and on, but what could you really say about Hef that hasn't already been mumbled incoherently by a thousand young women with his cock in their mouth? I've read just about every issue of *Playboy* since I was fifteen years old. Not once did I ever see a Playmate say one of her turn-ons was fucking a seventy-five-year-old man." This joke got roars from the crowd and a nod of agreement from Hefner.

The next to speak was funny *Saturday Night Live* alum Rob Schneider, whom Kimmel introduced as being "so short he doesn't even have to bend over to kiss Adam Sandler's ass." Rob was the first person of the night to address the topic that was foremost in everybody's mind. "If it were left up to the terrorists," he said, "women couldn't read, couldn't work, get fake tits, go to school, or pose nude to help their career. Hugh Hefner believes that women should be able to do all those things—except read."

Rob was doing great for a while, but then a few jokes in a row fell flat. The crowd's mood was already delicate, and as one of the producers of the show, I suddenly felt a need to try to help the situation. I ran up to the podium, put my arm around him, and said, "C'mon Rob, hasn't there been enough bombing in this city?" The crowd exploded into applause. Any tension in the room was now completely lifted and Hef's roasting was now coasting.

Some of my favorite moments were when Cedric the Entertainer stripped down to his silk pajamas in hopes of getting an invite to one of Hef's lingerie parties, when Adam Carolla cer-

ROB, ADAM, ME, AND JIMMY. AS SOON AS JIMMY
SAW ME WEARING BUDDY HACKETT'S COUNTRY-STYLE BOW TIE,
HE CALLED ME "THE KENTUCKY FRIED COMEDIAN."

emoniously presented his idol and the father of mainstream por-
nography with his high school jizz rag, when rapper Ice-T told the
audience he was only there "to rape all the white bitches," when
Drew Carey repeatedly called Osama bin Laden a "cunt," when
Alan King referred to the honoree as "a man who thinks the early
bird special is eating pussy before six o'clock," and when seventy-
seven-year-old Dick Gregory offered his gratitude to Mr. Hefner
for booking black comics in the Playboy Clubs during the days
of segregation. His voice rose as he said, "Hefner, you didn't give
me a lecture . . . you didn't give me instructions . . . you simply
had the courage back then to let blacks stand flat-footed and just
talk. . . . You let the world look at us and understand our genius,

so I came here today to thank you." Hef's eyes filled with tears. So did mine.

Then Mr. Gregory paid tribute to the American spirit during these tough times. "God and fear don't occupy the same space," he said before getting an emotional standing ovation. Right on cue Jimmy Kimmel leaped back up and said, "Someone forgot to tell Dick Gregory this was a roast," before launching into yet another hilarious joke about whacking off that I can't remember.

Moments earlier I had leaned over and whispered in Jimmy's ear that it might be interesting to riff with Hef's seven platinum blond girlfriends, who were sitting conveniently at a table right in front. Jimmy instantly took the bait. "You girls having fun? How does it work, do you put the dye in one big bathtub and stick your heads in all at once? You must save money that way, right?" This observation got exceptionally big laughs from the seven well-dressed beauties, who were more than happy to be part of the show.

One of the odder performances of the night was when the rubbery *In Living Color* alum Tommy Davidson grabbed the mic and went into his imitation of Sammy Davis Jr. singing "Candy Man." His big joke was that he switched the words from "Candy Man" to "Pussy Man" in honor of Hef's reputation as a world-class lothario. Mr. Hefner smiled politely even though this awkward bit clearly was not going over with the sophisticated Manhattan crowd. He's a very talented performer, but roasting isn't for everybody. By some miracle of good fortune (or because I helped make the lineup), I was the next roaster. My opening joke was, "Tommy Davidson, holy shit. If Sammy Davis Jr. were alive to see that he would've poked his other eye out!"

After my usual spritzing of the dais members ("Abe Vigoda, it's *Playboy,* not play dead!"), I eventually turned my attention to the guest of honor, whom I called a . . . "brave pioneer in the world of publishing." Then I followed it up with, "Actually, we were gonna get Larry Flynt, but nobody wanted to build a ramp." (Hef later told me that was his favorite joke of the night.)

Next I offered up some roasty reverence. "Mr. Hefner, I just want to say that you are my idol, but I don't even want an autograph. I just want to shake your dick. Let's face it, Hef has fondled more playmates than Michael Jackson." Then I mentioned how the first time I got asked to a party at the Playboy Mansion I was so excited, "I almost came on the invitation." I continued, "It was a benefit for Hef's favorite charity, Tits for Tots." The man of the hour giggled as I adjusted Buddy Hackett's bow tie and kept going. "Personally, Hef, I think it's awesome that you sleep with seven women because eight would be ostentatious. But look on the bright side, ladies . . . you only have to sleep on the wet spot once a week." (The girls high-fived on that one.) "By the way, Hef, one of your lovely girlfriends explained to me why you need seven women in bed. . . . One to put it in, and the other six to move you around." Then I took a bow and started drinking heavily.

The most memorable part of the night came at the very end, when the great Gilbert Gottfried closed the show. For reasons all the shrinks in Bellevue wouldn't be able to understand, Gilbert relishes in smashing through the boundaries of good taste. Being asked to close a Friars roast in the wake of a national tragedy suddenly gave the screaming Double G his greatest opportunity ever to piss people off.

Gilbert strode meekly up to the microphone wearing the type of white tuxedo jacket you might see on a waiter in a Chinese restaurant. Then he gripped the podium like he was about to take off and yelled, "Ice-T did my whole act so I'll do it anyway: I'm going to follow you white motherfuckers home and rape all you white bitches. . . ." Then he repeated this refrain about thirty times, to the delight of the audience. "You see, it's such a strong bit it still works," Gilbert said. Then with no segue whatsoever he said, "When Hugh Hefner is in bed with a woman, he can make her scream. . . . She screams out, 'Is he breathing!?' " Then he said, "But in all fairness to Mr. Hefner, he really had to fight for freedom of speech, so we could say things we couldn't say before. Like: 'Die, you senile old bastard! Die!' "

Gilbert was relentless. "Hugh Hefner is so old his first condom was made out of bark. Hugh Hefner invented a new sexual position called a ninety-six, where you turn around and fart on each other's head." Gilbert just continued bombarding the guest of honor with filthy jokes that I was too drunk to retain. I think

one was about Hef being so old he collects ice cream sticks and tapes them around his dick to use as a splint.

After about five minutes, Gilbert was finally warmed up and ready to cross the line. "Tonight I'll be using my Muslim name, Hasn't Been Laid. Which reminds me, I have a flight to California. I can't get a direct flight. They said they have to stop at the Empire State Building first." This remark was met by stunned silence. A few people even started hissing. A guy in the back yelled, "Too soon!" That's when Gilbert shrugged his shoulders and said, "Awwww . . . what the fuck do you care?" Now I started to hear a few boos. Gilbert got quiet and let them die down. Then he started to fidget around and flail his arms spastically. Was he having a seizure? Was he summoning some mystic comedy god? Or was he trying to pretend he didn't just do that joke about crashing into the Empire State Building? Nobody will ever know for sure, but my guess is that it was a combination of all three.

Finally, Gilbert started up again in a soft tone. "A talent agent is sitting in his office. A family walks in. A man, woman, two kids, their little dog, and the talent agent goes, 'What kind of an act do you do?' the father says, 'Let me show you . . .'" Then, according to Gilbert's telling, the family takes off their clothes and "the father starts fucking his wife and the wife starts jerking off the son. The son starts going down on the sister. The sister starts fingering the dog's asshole. Then the son starts blowing his father . . ."

At this point the crowd was laughing so hard I almost couldn't believe it. Rob Schneider literally fell out of his chair and started crawling around the floor gasping for air. "Want me to start at the beginning?" Gilbert screamed. But he didn't. He just kept going, turning this old joke into an epic discourse on shit, piss, come, blood, sweat, and bestiality.

"Then the son starts blowing the father . . . The daughter starts licking out the father's asshole . . . then the father shits on the floor . . . the mother shits on the floor . . . the dog shits and pisses on the floor . . . They all jump down into the shit and piss and come . . . and they start fucking and sucking each other . . ." Gilbert simply went on and on and on until the audience was not only laughing but uplifted.

After getting ten applause breaks and giving at least that many heart attacks to the older Friars, Gilbert finally decided we'd all had enough and he got to the punch line. "So then the family takes a bow and the talent agent says, 'Well, that's an interesting act,' which is kind of an understatement. 'What do you call your-selves?' And they say, 'The Aristocrats!' "

Gilbert's showstopping improvisation masterfully capped off a euphoric experience for everybody in attendance that night. When Hef finally accepted his elegant crystal Friars Club lifetime achievement award, he admitted, "I can't remember when I've had this much fun sitting up." Then in a voice quivering with emotion he added, "I'm glad I came—particularly at this time when this world needs a little laughter, so thank you and God bless you. I love you." Then Hef blew us all a kiss.

Some of the older Friars who were there say it was the greatest roast they had ever witnessed. Since there was no after-party, Ice-T took everybody out to a strip club. In the end, the New

York Friars Club Roast of Hugh Hefner raised $650,000 for the Twin Towers Fund (less the $800 we spent on lap dances).

Now every time I fly back into Manhattan I look out at the drastically altered skyline and can't help but think of that unforgettable roast; a momentary bright spot during our darkest days. Whatever type of gigantic retail complex they wind up building over Ground Zero, I hope it includes a comedy club—because that would be the ultimate fuck-you to the terrorists. Let freedom zing! Again!

OTHER GREAT LINES FROM THE GREATEST ROAST EVER

"Hef, I smell pussy. Did you burp?"   —Artie Lange

"Hef, when they write your name in the book of life I hope the pages aren't stuck together."—Rob Schneider

"Security is extremely tight tonight. As a matter of fact, I hear some of Hef's girls got frisked two or three times—and that was by Drew Carey."   —Me

"I wouldn't say Jimmy Kimmel's a hairy guy but Jeff Ross told me it took him twenty-five minutes to find his anus."   —Adam Carolla

"Black folks understand the greatness of America. Look at Michael Jackson . . . where else could a poor black boy born in utter poverty in Gary, Indiana, end up being a rich white man? Only in America!"
—Dick Gregory

"Dick Gregory—he deserves a round of applause just for being so old for his race."   —Sarah Silverman

"Alan King, a nursing home in Florida just called . . . the last person who thinks you're funny just died."
—Sarah Silverman

"Hef, thanks for letting us jack off to pictures of women you've already fucked."   —Drew Carey

"Hef has always been a sexual innovator. He was the first person to mix Viagra with prune juice. Now he doesn't know if he's comin' or goin'."   —Me

"Let's face it, the only way Hugh Hefner can get stiff is through rigor mortis—you white motherfuckers!"
—Gilbert Gottfried

A ROASTMASTER SHALL NOT WEAR FLIP-FLOPS

*T*HERE IS NOTHING MORE DISGUSTING than men's feet. I don't want to smell them. I don't want to touch them. And I sure as shoeshine don't want to look at them—especially while I'm performing.

Modern-day Roastmasters certainly don't need to roll around town wearing tuxedos like the Rat Pack once did—but they shouldn't be showing up places with their bunions, hangnails, hammertoes, blisters, fungus, and sickening black toenails fully exposed for our viewing displeasure. In fact, any fully grown man wearing flip-flops out in public during evening hours should be slapped and given a pair of socks. I don't care how nice you think your toes are, they are disgusting to other people. Plus, wearing flip-flops out at night is like saying to your buddies, "Hey, if anybody messes with us tonight, I'm not fighting. Sorry, but I just don't have the proper ankle support to throw down. You guys hug it out with these Crips while I flippity-flop the fuck home." So the next time you see a dude wearing flip-flops on a Saturday night, wink at his girlfriend. Unless he's a black belt in karate or carrying a gun, there ain't a damn thing he's gonna do about it.

Of course, the complete opposite is true for women. Men love seeing women's feet and I myself have often wondered if I don't have some sort of fetish. In fact, if given the chance to smooch my girlfriend on the body part of my choosing, I'll usually pick those ten little piggies. I especially like pink nail polish. No doubt such disclosures will come back to haunt me if I am ever the subject of a roast.

But that might not happen for a long time. After all, roasts are rare and special occasions. Therefore, I always encourage participants to break out their most royal duds. Since these events are usually associated with vulgarities and debauchery, I feel it is a Roastmaster's duty to class up the joint.

MY DAD LOOKING SHARP AS ALWAYS.

When I heard Comedy Central was roasting rap legend and reality star Flavor Flav, I knew I had to do something special with my wardrobe. My dad always dressed to impress. He felt it was important to show his brides and grooms at the catering hall that he cared about their parties as much as they did. I think the same principle applies to show business. If the performer doesn't care about the show, why should the audience?

Clearly I couldn't roast someone as outlandish as Flavor Flav wearing tired attire. I had to represent for my old high school pals back in Jersey, who were all big Public Enemy fans back in the day. My last year of high school, my pal Haimo bought himself a gigantic menacing Oldsmobile 98, and my homeys and I would cruise around all night blasting the voices of Chuck D, Flavor Flav, and Terminator X into the suburban Jersey sky, *"Suckers to the side I know you hate my 98 . . . You gonna get yours!"* I'm still not sure what that meant, but it sounded cool and didn't seem to have anything to do with killing whitey. To us rebellious punk rockers, Public Enemy was The Clash of the hip-hop world. By the time "Fight the Power" arrived as the anthem to Spike Lee's film *Do the Right Thing,* I was probably their single biggest Caucasian fan. For me, roasting Flavor Flav some twenty years later would be a thrill.

I went to a dozen stores on two coasts in search of just the right shade of hot pink dress shirt to wear with my new black Paul Smith suit and matching fedora. In my closet, I also discovered a hot pink silk hankie that belonged to my dad. Producer Joel Gallen presented me with a custom-made drinking chalice that said "Roastmaster General" in diamonds. The night of the roast I sat proudly on that dais looking like some sort of high-class pimp-caterer.

Still, I didn't look quite as à la mode as rapping roaster Snoop Dogg, who wore a light gold hoodie to match his solid gold bicycle chain necklace. Along with his gold chalice and gold sneakers, Snoop was the night's best dressed and the funniest. Coincidence? No fucking way. Looking suave gave him a certain swagger that helped his performance. He stepped to the podium and broke it down. "The haters got the nerve to come up here and try and

diss me / but I'm an original and Flav is extra crispy. He's dried out, ashy, and wishes he was taller / Flav, you look like one of my blunts, except smaller."

After Snoop, Jimmy Kimmel, Ice-T, Greg Geraldo, Patton Oswalt of *Ratatouille* fame, and a few others took their shots at the hype man of the hour, it was my turn. The evening's Roast-master Katt Williams introduced me as if he were reading a ran-som note. He clearly feared me. He knew I was about to bring the pain. I removed my hat, placed my diamond-encrusted kiddush cup on the podium, and began. . . .

"C'mon folks, keep it going for D. L. Ugly!"

The diminutive Katt was not amused. I tried not to think about the fact that he had recently been arrested for gun posses-sion. "Katt Williams . . . Flavor Flav . . . What is this, a telethon for black leprechauns?" Any second I could get shot in the knees.

"Couldn't they cough up another thirty bucks and get Bush-wick Bill up in this bitch?"

Katt ran offstage to hide, or possibly get a gun . . . I kept going after him anyway.

"But Katt, wherever you are, I want you to know you're doing a great job as tonight's Roastmaster—but you gotta admit you are a very weird-looking dude. You look like Snoop Dogg and Rata-touille had a baby."

At this point I felt confident I might not be assassinated be-cause Snoop and Flavor Flav were literally falling off their thrones. "What are you laughing at, Flav? You look like Whoopi Goldberg and Gollum from *Lord of the Rings* had an abortion."

Flav kicked his legs in the air in appreciation. The place went nuts. I pleaded to the audience, "This is impossible! How do you embarrass a crackhead who wears a Viking helmet? Look at him—he has forty kids and three teeth. Seriously, Flav, you really are the ugliest man in America. How do you roast charcoal? Starving children send him fifty cents a day!"

The crowd applauded. Then I took a quick break from roasting for a boasting. "I'm in it to win it, motherfuckers!" To fill the time while the crowd cheered I took out my dad's hot pink hankie and pretended to wipe the sweat from my brow.

"Flav, I'm sorry, but I didn't watch your show, *Flavor of Love* . . . I dunno . . . it's not my thing . . . If I wanna see a midget bang a bunch of hookers I'll go to a party at Jeremy Piven's house." (I'll admit this was a low blow because Jeremy Piven wasn't in attendance. I just liked the joke so much I had to say it. Plus, he's one of my favorite actors.)

"Flav, when white people watch your show they say, 'Hey, this guy's hilarious.' When black people watch your show they say, 'I hope no white people are watching this right now.' Let's face it, Flav, you set African-Americans back twenty years and you set Viking Americans back seven hundred fifty years. But I gotta give it up to ya, Flav—you are a ladies' man. You probably slept with more hot black chicks than Robert De Niro and Thomas Jefferson combined." (This joke eventually got cut from the TV broadcast, but I still thought it was pretty good.)

Then I looked out in the crowd and spotted two tables where Flav's *Flavor of Love* reality-show slutestants were seated. These women lived in a penthouse with Flavor Flav and competed for his affections. Each week Flav kicked somebody out until he was left alone with his true love. The winner got $100,000 and the disease of her choosing. I decided to get down and dirty with these women. I knew my suave appearance would carry me through a rare plunge into scatological humor.

"Now let's give it up for all Flav's ladies here tonight . . . I see Deelishis, Saaphyri, and of course, there's the lovely young lady who crapped on the rug." (A reference to an actual defecation that took place on Flav's reality show.) "Flav was confused by that. He thought she was giving birth to his baby."

Of course, Flav's ladies loved the attention. They started throwing kisses and spreading germs.

"Damn, Flav, what do you think of all these gold teeth diggers?"

Flav happily blurted out his trademark phrases, "Yeah, Boy-eeeeee!" and "Flava Flaaaaaav!" to thunderous applause. Riding his energy, I continued. "What a hot ghetto mess we got in here tonight! Ya know, ladies, I heard Flav's teeth aren't actually gold . . . they just decayed from eating all your nasty pussies." (I know, a groaner. But I recovered quickly.) "Ladies, it's time to start thinking positive—H.I.V. positive. Let's face it—there were so many yeast infections in that house you could've opened a Pinkberry."

Then I leaned on the podium and got serious for a second. "But I gotta tell ya, Flav—back in the day I was the world's biggest Public Enemy fan. Me and my pals would cruise around listening to 'Fight the Power' . . . 'Our freedom of speech is freedom or death . . . We gotta fight the powers that be!' That was awesome. Now look at you. You sold out quicker than the iPhone!" (Because of this joke Comedy Central sent me an iPhone as a gift afterward.)

"But seriously, Flav, you're like family to me. In fact, you remind me of my uncle—my Uncle Tom." This was a risky joke—but since Flav fell on the floor writhing with laughter, I figured he was okay with it. Ice-T and Snoop picked him up and put him back on his throne as I continued.

"Don't worry, I know these are sensitive times—and I'm not gonna do racial humor—besides, the fact that Flav is black is like the fifth thing that's wrong with him." (Biggest laugh of the night and one of my favorite roast jokes ever. Partially because it was told in the ugly wake of Michael Richards's "n-word" controversy. I wanted to demonstrate that loaded subjects are okay—as long as they are handled by competent professionals.)

"Hey, we all know Flav loves stickin' it to the white man— and that white man is Brigitte Nielsen." (Cut to Brigitte Nielsen, who is seven feet tall and looks like a robot hooker.)

"Take a bow, babe. Wow, I think we know who wore the condom in their relationship . . . nobody! Uch, I'd rather fuck Leslie Nielsen. What did you do, Brigitte—use Flav as a dildo? But tonight, Flav, it's all about you and your amazing career . . . five gold records, three reality shows, and two bronze medals from the Special Olympics."

Finally, I lifted my chalice in a toast. "Anyway, this has been fun—and it's all been for a good cause—child support! Feed the children! L'Chaim!"

Not only did I not get shot that night but I absolutely murdered. Dressing up helps me get away with more dangerous material. A layer of sophistication, I believe, enhances any risqué performance. Plus, there is nothing more fun than *dressing to kill*—and then killing. Yeah, Boyeeeeeee! Flaaaaaaaava Flav!! What a business. How does this toothless mental patient get rich banging hos and I gotta stay up all night writing down roasting secrets for my future competition? I hope you appreciate this, you lucky motherfuckers.

A ROASTMASTER
MUST SPREAD THE LOVE

*W*HILE ROASTING YOU DON'T *ONLY* have to make fun of the guest of honor. Once a guest agrees to sit on the dais at a roast, they automatically become fair game. Whether they admit it or not, everyone wants to be part of the show. Plus, making fun of them reduces your chance of having material similar to the other roasters'. After all, how many bad hair jokes about Donald Trump can one audience really tolerate? Okay . . . bad example . . .

The ancient thespian Abe Vigoda comes to every single Friars Club roast and each time I remind the audience that he's either dead or dying. At the Drew Carey roast I said, "Drew, this really is a special night. My one regret is that Abe Vigoda isn't alive to see this." The cameras cut to poor Abe looking completely oblivious, which of course tripled the laugh. So as not to appear like I was piling on, I crafted my next joke to seem like it was about the guest of honor even though it was really just another one about Abe. "Drew, you're a big gambler: Tell me, what's the over/under on Abe Vigoda?" Then I reached my hand out toward the audience and demonstrated the secret Friars Club handshake, which is really just a regular handshake delivered shakily.

Age jokes run rampant at every roast. After all, there is always *somebody* who is the oldest bastard in the room. Therefore, you

TWO UGLY MUGS.

can never have too many near-death–themed putdowns at the ready. Here's a helpful exercise: Think of the oldest person you know and try to come up with two or three disparaging things to say about them. Some useful angles include associating them with historical events or chronic incontinence. Then wait till you're with them at a party or family dinner and deliver the jokes as if they were off the top of your head. Not only will you liven up the gathering, everybody will think you're a genius.

Abe Vigoda is the oldest guy I know, and crafting morbid cracks about him has become a favorite hobby of mine. Not all of them are home runs and many of them don't even make sense, but they are a blast to write. In fact, at movie director Rob Reiner's roast I wrote more stuff about Abe than I did about the guest of honor. "It's always nice to see my pal Abe Vigoda—or, as he's known in the hip-hop community, Vanilla Ice Age. That's right, Abe is hard-core gangsta. Backstage I saw him doing shots of formaldehyde. Poor Abe, I hear he's addicted to drugs. Mostly stool softeners. Let's face it—Abe Vigoda is so old they revoked his donor card. His blood type is O-shit. But in all honesty, Abe is keeping very busy. I hear he's about to star in a sequel of *I Know What You Did Last Summer* called *I Forgot What I Did Five Minutes Ago*."

Sometimes I can't stop myself. Once while roasting Jerry Lewis, I randomly turned to Abe Vigoda right in the middle of my speech and said, "Hang in there, Abe—we're just looking for a sixth pallbearer." At journalist Matt Lauer's roast I took a more somber approach. I simply bowed my head and requested "a moment of silence for our dear friend, Abe Vigoda." Then in a reference to Matt Lauer's popular travel segments on *The Today Show* I said, "Poor Abe Vigoda doesn't even know 'where in the world' *he* is right now. C'mon, Abe—don't you think it's finally time to change your Facebook status to 'Resting in Peace'?"

The truth is, I love the guy and I hope he lives forever. Then I could write a whole book of jokes about him entitled *The Death & Times of Abe Vigoda*. Still, he cannot brag that he has been my most harshly abused dais victim. That honor goes to none other than the funniest comedic actress of all time—the late great Miss Beatrice Arthur. But rather than a backlog of jokes doled out over the course of a decade, I clobbered this poor woman with just one powerful A-bomb sucker punch from left field. Some say it was my greatest roast moment ever. I beg to agree.

It all started when she showed up at a roast for her dear friend Jerry Stiller, who had recently reached sitcom superstar status playing Jason Alexander's dad on *Seinfeld* and Kevin James's father-in-law on *King of Queens*.

Not only was I one of the roasters, I was also one of the show's producers. This meant I had to be especially nice to everybody—at least until the show started.

In the days leading up I would usually listen to everybody's material and make suggestions and offer up any joke tags that popped into my head. Also, if somebody had doubts about the offensiveness of a joke, they would usually run it by me. I like to consider myself a good barometer of what is and isn't over the line.

About halfway through the show, the comedienne slash actress slash nightmare Sandra Bernhard got up and sang "Magic Man" by the band Heart, while giving a lap dance to a nauseous-looking Jerry Stiller. Many audience members covered their eyes in horror. As I sat there waiting to go on next, my mind searched for something to say about Sandra's off-putting performance. Finally it hit me. But the punch line wasn't really about my fellow Friar Sandra Bernhard, it was about the woman sitting next to her, Bea Arthur, whom I had never even met. Of course, I'm a huge fan of both *Maude* and *Golden Girls,* and the idea of working such a revered star into my routine seemed absolutely titillating.

However, I quickly realized that this joke that had popped into my head was probably over the line. I ran it by Jimmy Kimmel and Kevin James. They both told me not to do it. Still, I figured if I was killing, I could *maaaaaybe* pull it off—so I wrote it down in the margin of my notes anyway.

It was finally my turn. The capable Roastmaster Jason Alexander attempted to slam me for being ugly and unsuccessful, but I promptly took the podium and put him in his place . . . "Jason Alexander, you were great on *Seinfeld*—and I guess that's gonna be about it, huh? You sing, you dance, you act . . . you do everything except make people laugh." Next I couldn't resist a joke about the absence of Jerry Seinfeld, who "wanted to be here but he had a prior engagement to fuck a model on a pile of cash."

Then, of course, I needed to get my obligatory Abe Vigoda crowd-pleasers out of the way. "Before I begin I need to make an announcement: Abe Vigoda asked me to invite everybody to his funeral taking place on November ninth at the Museum of Natural History. Please call Abe to RSVP. In lieu of flowers, donations can be made to Larry Storch."

I was warmed up and ready to go after some heavy hitters. Ben Stiller was sitting with his good friend and frequent collaborator Janeane Garofalo. Their new movie, *Mystery Men,* had just crashed and burned in theaters on the opening weekend. The subject was ripe so I went for it. "Janeane Garofalo, let me give you some career advice . . . you're allowed to turn things down. Just say 'No.' You're a great actress, but let's face it, pal—you're responsible for more shitty pictures than Fotomat. Your last movie left the theaters so fast they held the premiere at a Blockbuster. And the movie you just made with Ben? *Mystery Men?* C'mon, that movie was so bad, I fired my agent." The cameras cut to Ben Stiller. He nodded his head and mouthed the words "I should've fired mine," which made the joke funnier because, like a true professional, he was playing the moment. Then I said, "Folks, Gene Siskel was gonna review that movie, but he decided to take the easy way out." Of course, this was a reference to the popular movie critic, who had recently passed away. I had written the joke while on the phone with Buddy Hackett the night before and I figured if this absurdly insensitive line got a big laugh, which it did, then I could probably get away with the killer Sandra Bernhard/Bea Arthur joke scribbled in my margin.

I glanced down the dais. Bea Arthur seemed to be enjoying herself. Still, I wasn't ready to go for it. Instead, I turned my attention to a less intimidating target—Dr. Ruth Westheimer, the diminutive sex therapist who, I declared, "is so old her vagina has mice" and "she lost her virginity to a Cossack." Then I finished her off with a line Uncle Miltie lent me just for the occasion. "Doctor Ruth, you look like a million dollars—all green and crumpled."

I was starting to feel almost too confident. I spotted New York City's police commissioner Howard Safir sitting a few seats down. I couldn't believe such an important city official was brave enough to sit on the dais of a Friars roast—especially considering his office was currently under fire due to the recent sodomizing of a Haitian immigrant named Abner Louima with a plunger handle in a police station men's room.

DR. RUTH, ME, AND JANEANE GAROFALO IN A PRE-ROAST TABLEAU.

In the sweetest voice possible I said, "New York City Police Commissioner Howard Safir is here. Howard, hold up your plunger so people know who you are exactly." To his credit, the police commissioner looked relieved to be having a laugh about the incident. I like to think of that roast moment as one of my boldest ever. However, it is certainly not the most remembered. That distinction goes to the very next joke I said that night. I looked out at Sandra Bernhard, who had only moments ago creeped everybody out with her risqué performance, and said, "Sandra Bernhard— holy shit, I wouldn't fuck you with Bea Arthur's dick!"

Gasp. Bea Arthur, who had obviously been caught totally off-guard, leered at me for a very long time. The crowd burst into a laugh that seemed to last four minutes. The entire time Bea Arthur was pointing at me threateningly as if to say, "You're dead meat, kid." Sure, my joke was funny. But her icy reaction turned it into a roast masterpiece.

What I'm saying is, don't just tell the jokes—play the moments. Remember, it's not just what you're saying that is funny, it is also how the person you're talking about reacts to it that makes it work. For instance, the only way to get away with telling Donald Trump that "it looked like a raccoon died on his head" was because he was laughing the hardest. If you are teasing a good sport, anything goes.

Still, Bea Arthur's evil stink eye was so convincing that I wasn't sure if I had actually pissed her off or not. But I couldn't worry about that now, I had to move on. After all, we weren't there to roast Bea Arthur, we were there to roast Jerry Stiller ". . . or, as the network brass calls him, The Hunchback of CBS. Let's face it, Jerry Stiller has the face of a star! And that star is Lassie. When Jerry Stiller walked into Makeup, I heard one makeup person say to the other, 'Call your insurance, this one's totaled.' "

Jerry's longtime wife and even longer-time comedy partner, Anne Meara, was in attendance also. Back in the day, Stiller and Meara had made more than one hundred appearances on *The Ed Sullivan Show*, so I certainly didn't want to leave her out. "And what about the great comedy team of Stiller and Meara? A comedy team Americans grew up watching until they were old enough to realize they weren't funny. The only time I saw Stiller and Meara perform live was at Henny Youngman's funeral. Henny was funnier. That reminds me . . . hey, Abe—I owe Henny Youngman twenty bucks. Do you mind paying him for me when you see him?"

Finally, I whipped out a poem I'd written for the occasion called "The Wrong Jerry." The lights dimmed and the orchestra accompanied me as I recited. "We could've roasted Seinfeld or Springer, Vale or Van Dyke. Any Jerry'd be better than this crabby old kike. When the Friars called me I nearly went spastic; any Jerry'd be better than this one-note geriatric. I'll admit when I saw you on *Seinfeld*—I thought you were super. But I heard a rumor: their first choice? Pat Cooper! Jerry, all jokes aside—and this thought is my last . . . Thank you for this chance—to kiss your son's ass."

Sure, I finished up nice, but certainly nothing could truly follow that explosive Bea Arthur moment. As soon as the show was over, I tried to make my way over to her so I could properly introduce myself and thank her for being such a good sport. But she was gone—nowhere to be seen. Eventually the roast aired on television, and for months afterward, a day didn't go by when somebody didn't ask me about "Bea Arthur's dick." Somehow this silly and not particularly clever line had become the most famous roast moment in modern times. One fan even sent me a giant dildo with Bea Arthur's face painted on the tip. I sleep with it under my pillow just in case I am attacked during the night.

Poor Bea. I figured that if I was hearing about the joke this much, then she must be too. I wondered if she was okay with it. Finally, after nearly two years of people constantly mentioning Bea Arthur's dick everywhere I went, I decided I had to track her down and thank her for making me famous.

I did some Googling and Yahooing and discovered that she was currently touring the country in a one-man show called *An Evening with Bea Arthur.* Turns out it was coming to Los Angeles in a few weeks, so I bought a ticket.

As expected, her show was sold out and very compelling. Standing alone and barefoot onstage with only piano accompaniment, Bea Arthur shared her show business anecdotes and sang some of the great songs from *Mame* and *Fidder on the Roof* that she had first sung on Broadway. Afterward, I stood in a very long line of fans waiting to meet her, with a bouquet of flowers in hand. I purposely went to the very end because I did not want this important encounter to be rushed. Finally, it was my turn. Holding the flowers, I approached cautiously and said, "Miss Arthur, I don't know if you remember me, but we met at Jerry Stiller's roast and—"

"—And you nailed me, you prick!" she said, cutting me off. She knew exactly who I was and we both cracked up. Then I said, "I just wanted to thank you for being a good sport that night—and to tell you that your show tonight was fantastic. These are for you." I handed her the flowers. She took them and smiled at me. I was so relieved. She seemed totally fine with the whole thing. She even asked me back to her dressing room to meet her friends, but when we got back there everybody was on the way out. The elegant show business legend told me to sit down and handed me a glass of merlot.

Over the next couple of hours we drank and told each other stories from our lives. I was surprised to learn that she was once in the Marines. I told her about how when I was little my parents used to argue a lot, but that when her first sitcom, *Maude,* came on, everybody in my house stopped yelling at each other and gathered around the TV as a family. Bea told me about how she used to go to the *Golden Girls* set half an hour early on tape days so she could make her costar Rue McClanahan crazy by sneaking into her trailer and leaving a big unflushed dump in the toilet. Ah, the glamour of Hollywood.

After sharing two bottles of wine and many more secrets, I

was ready to bring this amazing night to a close. As I got up to leave, Bea pushed me back down onto the sofa. I thought she was joking until she grabbed my head with her big hands and planted a wet kiss on my mouth. She even tried to slip me the tongue. When I tried to get up she pushed me down again and clapped out the lights. Before I even knew what was going on, Bea flipped me over, yanked my pants down, and shoved SOMETHING in my you-know-what. But there was no use fighting it. I was hers. At one point she told me to "shut up and take it like a man."

We made love for hours. I'd never been with a woman twice my age, but a Roastmaster must be open to new experiences. Our bodies had a symbiotic relationship—like a new baseball inside a well-worn catcher's mitt. Since I'm a gentleman, and so is she, I won't tell you what happened after she took her teeth out. She even let me videotape some juicy moments for posterity. One day

I'll release the footage to the world, but for now this will have to be our little secret. A Roastmaster never brags—but I just *had* to tell somebody.

Now, like all of us, I am left with only my memories of her. She is gone, but certainly not forgotten. I can only hope she died with an erection. I miss you, Queen Bea.

A ROASTMASTER HAS A BACKSTAGE PASS TO THE WORLD

*O*NE GREAT PERK OF BEING a Roastmaster is that you get the occasional invitation to a place that mere mortals don't get to experience. Such invites usually have something to do with sports, music, or entertainment. I've been on the field at Yankee Stadium during the World Series. I've done shots of Jägermeister in the Foo Fighters' dressing room. I've been in the grotto at the Playboy Mansion. Those are the festive ones. But other locales are not so full of baseballs, booze, or boners. Some are even quite scary—such as the terrorist prison in Guantánamo Bay, Cuba, where I was once invited to perform stand-up.

Gitmo—it's a name that immediately sends a chill up your spine, like "Transylvania" or "Clay Aiken." As much as I love performing for our men and women in uniform, the opportunity to perform at Gitmo seemed to pose at least a mild moral quandary. The interrogation tactics reputedly used there struck me as nightmarish, inhumane, and wholly without basis in decency or good taste—and this is coming from a guy who has voluntarily appeared on *The View* eleven times.

Of course, I've performed in depressing places before and undoubtedly will again—but the crappiest comedy club is still a lot better than a torture dungeon for wannabe shoe bombers, located on a spider-infested beach and guarded by grim-faced men with machine guns. So when the invitation came, I was on the barbed-wire fence about it. But then I realized I'd be a fool to decline a chance to see with my own eyes what this mysterious, possibly evil place was actually like.

So my mind was made up to go, but I knew I couldn't go alone. But whom to take? The choices were endless but unsatisfactory. A *Playboy* Playmate? Too distracting. The Foo Fighters? Too much equipment. Then it hit me like a cell phone thrown at my head by Naomi Campbell. I decided to bring along more comedians, because surely it would take more than me to brighten the mood at this godforsaken gulag. This was clearly a triple headliner mission.

I convinced two of my funniest pals—the smooth-as-silk Tony Woods and the sick-ass fuck Jim Norton—to come with me by telling them this was a rare opportunity to be a witness to history. Plus, we'd be transported there via a top-of-the-line, state-of-the-art spy plane that would make us feel like we were in a James Bond movie.

We left on a Friday at the crack of noon. For the entire bumpy flight, Jim and Tony looked at me like they were going to throw me off with no flotation device but my own belly to save me. The plane wasn't something out of a James Bond movie. It was something out of a silent movie. This thing was so old, Orville Wright took a piss in the bathroom. We ate our military lunch in rusty bucket seats, concentrating intently on not puking or soiling ourselves as the plane rattled, lurched, wheezed, and panted its way through the sky and into Cuban airspace.

Upon landing we were herded like nauseous cattle onto a rickety boat, giving us the unique opportunity to barf from both air- and seasickness simultaneously. What a relief to finally arrive at our destination—a beautiful Caribbean beach, where high-value Al Qaeda terrorists are held under the tightest, scariest security imaginable. Let's party!

We were greeted by a senior naval officer, who looked like she hadn't cracked a smile since before the Cuban Missile Crisis. As military police examined our passports, she explained some basic Gitmo rules to us. We weren't allowed to take pictures of anything other than each other and we would not be permitted to visit with the detainees. I said, "Aw shucks, I was hoping to get Ramzi Bin al Shibh's autograph for my nephews!" Still no smile. In fact, her face seemed to become slightly more expressionless. Then they searched our luggage for well over an hour. What could I possibly be sneaking in—some unregistered puns?

While waiting in the blazing sun, Tony, Jim, and I debated Gitmo's many moral conundrums. Can torture ever be justified? Do terrorists have the same legal rights as POWs? Which one of us would look best in an orange jumpsuit? Of course, none of these questions had easy answers. There was one thing all three of us could agree on—it must suck to be a soldier stationed down here. Looking around we realized that other than the occasional iguana humping your leg, there couldn't be a whole lot to write home about at a place like Gitmo. Tony shook his head and said, "I've seen pictures of naked prisoners being dragged around on doggy leashes and forced to wear women's underwear."

"Sounds like a Tuesday afternoon at Jim Norton's house," I said.

Jimbo liked this idea and squealed with delight. "Ooh, ooh, good idea! Somebody detain me!"

When security finally finished sniffing my Underoos, a military vehicle picked us up and took us on a tour of beautiful downtown Gitmo. For a place with such a dreary reputation, parts of the one-hundred-year-old naval base were surprisingly idyllic. Sprinklers spraying well-manicured lawns in perfect tandem, school-bound kids on bikes waving good-bye to their moms— it brought to mind the manufactured tranquility of *The Truman Show*. There was even a McDonald's and a makeshift Starbucks, further reinforcing a sense of normalcy.

But then there was the prison looming in the distance, covered with dark clouds and concertina wire. It was originally built

so that the military would have an offshore place to hold Taliban fighters captured in Afghanistan in the wake of 9/11. By keeping them off U.S. soil and labeling them "enemy combatants" instead of "prisoners of war," the CIA had been able to hold many of them here indefinitely. Of course, this is a controversial policy that prompts human rights groups, some foreign governments, and many Americans to regularly call for the prison at Gitmo to be closed.

The base commander took us for a look-see. The atmosphere was eerie and quiet, as an armored Humvee slowly escorted us in wide serpentine patterns through three separate checkpoints. At the last checkpoint our cameras were taken away.

Inside the prison's cafeteria, a small group of guards was assembled to have lunch with us. I noticed that nobody wore name tags on their uniforms. When I asked a guard about this, he told me it was because they didn't want the detainees to know their true identities for fear of repercussions against their families back home. He then explained to me that of the roughly two hundred and fifty prisoners held at Gitmo, more than thirty of them are considered among the most dangerous men in the world. In fact, this particular building housed many of Osama bin Laden's personal bodyguards and numerous people trained in explosives, poisons, and disguises. *Wow—explosives, poisons, and disguises,* I thought. *Reminds me of the time I helped Carrot Top pack for spring break.*

After lunch we drove right up to the border fence, got out, and stared at the Cuban soldiers, who were already staring back at us. From a long distance, I could see them high on their posts watching our every move through binoculars in the 103-degree heat. I, however, had to keep looking down at the ground because there were some very gross, red creepy-crawly things running all over my new Adidas shell toes. Despite these awful conditions, a small rotation of marines stands guard at this fence twenty-four hours a day in the hope that the Cuban people will one day rush the perimeter in search of their freedom. Of course, the Cuban guards stand there ready to shoot anybody who dares to try.

Our show that night was in the Windjammer Lounge, which is the only bar on the base. The place was packed to the gills with the entire nonimprisoned Gitmo community, which consists mostly of sailors, marines, CIA agents, and their well-paid Arabic translators. I was hosting the show, so I went on first.

My strategy was to get the soldiers on my side with a little of what I like to call "vicarious insubordination." I do this by roasting the commanding officer on their behalf. I opened by saying, "Hey, Colonel, thanks so much for polishing not only your boots—but your head for the big show."

The crowd was supercharged. They were laughing so hard at my setups I didn't even get to the punch lines. The crowd went especially nuts when I made local references, such as one about that rinky-dink Starbucks I'd spotted on base. "They got a new drink you guys gotta try . . . five shots of espresso . . . then they throw water on you and punch you in the face. It's called a Whack-accino."

Next I went after the over-the-top security procedures at Gitmo, "They confiscated my cigar cutter! What am I gonna do, circumcise the detainees?"

I then asked a big hairy guard if they paid him extra to "bark at the prisoners." When I asked a marine in the front row with particularly big ears if he was a part of "Special-ed Forces" the gales of laughter capsized two fishing boats out in the bay.

Then I brought up one of the Middle Eastern translators, who happened to be wearing a Hawaiian shirt, and I told everybody he was Osama bin Laden's former masseuse. Everybody cracked up, including poor "Magic Fingers Farook" himself. This audience was so starved for chuckles they would've eaten a clown.

After making fun of nearly every person in attendance, I finally introduced my fellow Jersey joke-slinger, the eternally horny Jim Norton, who opened with a reference to the on-base restaurant they had taken us to for lunch earlier in the day, "You know how depressed I got when I saw that The Jerkhouse was a chicken joint?" I can't remember anything else Jim said, because I was laughing so hard I couldn't breathe, see, or think straight—it was like being water-boarded. I'm pretty sure he did an encore.

Then I went back up one more time and introduced the

classy but nasty Tony Woods. Tony was the perfect comedian for this crowd. Not only does he have hilarious stories about his time in the navy working as a dental hygienist, but his dark sense of humor was well suited for this crowd of warped souls. After staying onstage for nearly two hours, Tony finally closed with an elaborate and detailed routine about fucking a midget that had the crowd begging for mercy.

It was one of the best shows I'd ever been a part of. But afterward there were no Cuban cigars with which to celebrate. The commanding officer informed us that it was illegal for American citizens to smoke Cuban cigars *even* if they did it in Cuba. But as a gift for coming, he did present me with an American flag that had been flown over the base. I was very touched by this thoughtful gesture as we took our final bows to a standing ovation. Afterward we hung out with the soldiers until the Windjammer staff politely kicked us out.

That night as I lay in my bunk after six mojitos, two Claritins, and half a Dominican cigar, my mind drifted off into a fantastical dream where I imagined myself called to duty at Gitmo. I heard a cold, bureaucratic voice say, "Roastmaster General, your jokes have just barely passed the standards set forth by the Geneva Convention. We need you to roast a top Al Qaeda operative immediately. It's a matter of national security. You must not hold back."

In my mind I saw a disheveled Yemenese fanatic strapped to a dais, struggling helplessly while I did my thing at the podium. "Wow. Tough crowd—remind me never to follow an interrogation. What's the matter, Tariq? Did you wake up on the wrong side of the cave this morning? They say you were planning another 9/11 . . . but you don't look smart enough to work at a 7-Eleven."

Finally, the detainee's ears started bleeding and he screamed, "No! No! Make the ugly Jew stop! This is worse than sleep deprivation! I will tell you everything!" Then he broke through his restraints and lunged toward me, screaming in subtitles, "But first I'm going to kill this hacky infidel!" I thrashed so violently in my sleep that Jim and Tony finally woke me up.

"Bad nightmare, doll?" Jimbo asked.

"I dreamt my act was considered torture," I told him, wiping the sweat from my forehead.

"You weren't dreaming," he said.

In the end, despite my tropical and ethical misgivings, I'm proud I went to Gitmo and I'm thankful for the experience. The men and women I met there were goodhearted and more in need of a laugh than most. After all, being a Roastmaster isn't about politics—it's about people.

TONGUE LASHING

Military crowds are the most sophisticated, diverse, and appreciative that I encounter. So as you can imagine, roasting my childhood hero, Gene Simmons from KISS, to benefit wounded soldiers was a very cool opportunity. There were many injured heroes in attendance that night. I applauded them and asked Gene who he thought would win in a fight, "the army who defends freedom—or the army who defends 'Lick It Up?'" That night I relentlessly attacked Gene's inflated ego and legendary sexcapades. I said, "What a life! 103 million records. 4,800 women. Two friends. Let's face it, Gene Simmons is such an asshole that his own asshole changed its name to Murray. Interesting fact—Gene was born in Israel. Hey, maybe if he had stayed there the Palestinians wouldn't want the land back so bad. You soldiers want peace in the Middle East? Send this schmuck back to the Promised Land! What happened to ya, Gene? You used to rock and roll all night and party every day. Now you get up six times a night to go to the bathroom. Gene used to spit blood. Now he shits it." The demon rocker was actually a great sport and the soldiers in attendance truly appreciated him. During Gene's last licks he dropped his rock star 'tude and made a heartfelt speech that brought tears to his eyes—which he was able to wipe away with his freakishly long tongue.

A ROASTMASTER SHOULD NEVER TRUST WILLIE NELSON

OLKS ALWAYS ASK ME, "WHO was your favorite person to roast?" I always say, "Whoever's next." Preparing for a roast is something I really enjoy and take very seriously. Every new roast subject becomes my passion during the preparatory process. For Flavor Flav, I listened to all my old Public Enemy albums. For William Shatner, I watched tons of *Star Trek*. For Pam Anderson, I did a lot of Roastmasterbating. But never was I more thrilled about doing my research than in the case of legendary country-and-western singer and tax evader Willie Nelson.

Believe it or not, the seventy-eight-year-old singer-songwriter is a beloved icon among comedians. He's a logical hero for us if you think about it. For starters, most funnymen love weed and hate paying taxes. Willie's signature song "On the Road Again" is a touring comic's anthem for obvious reasons. Plus, Willie is so emaciated, pigtailed, and pathetic-looking that he doesn't threaten our masculinity like so many barrel-chested Southern troubadours. He's sort of a cross between Johnny Cash and Pippi

Longstocking. Willie's just so tiny and stoned and bumpkinly, I've always wanted to roast him.

Therefore, when I first heard the news that he agreed to be in the hot seat for the Comedy Central Roast in 2008, I nearly jumped for joy. I didn't actually jump, because I was taking a shit and smoking a joint while listening to "Blue Eyes Crying in the Rain" when I got the call. It was kismet!

To prepare, I immediately bought a fresh bag of weed and booked a four-night stay at a bed-and-breakfast in the Ozarks. In order to get in touch with my inner Willie, I wanted to journey deep into the hairy, toothless, yodeling heart of America, where I could soak up some of the bucolic atmosphere in order to make my roast more personal and authentic. That's a true Roastmaster's process: soak and then joke.

Imagine my disappointment when, not long after that, before I could even depart for my sojourn to the boonies, Willie up and canceled. Apparently he got cold feet. I was so roastfallen, I smashed my Willie Nelson vinyls and smoked all of my marijuana. I even called my accountant Harvey and started going over my 1099s.

As a fan, I was deeply hurt when Willie backed out. But a Roastmaster doesn't get bitter; a Roastmaster gets even. So, with all due respect and admiration: Fuck you, Willie. I'm roasting you here in this book.

This is an honor for me, Willie. Never before have I roasted a stoner from the Stone Age. He was also scheduled to appear at the Hollywood Bowl, but he smoked it instead. Willie smokes so much weed he buys his rolling paper at Costco.

I hear Willie once got so high he accidentally fucked someone he wasn't related to. What a ladies' man this guy is—I hear he has a different cousin in every city.

But contrary to popular belief, his parents weren't brother and sister. They were Adam and Eve. What an American institution. Willie Nelson was playing country music before we were a country. I heard he wrote "On the Road Again" while on tour with Lewis and Clark. Let's face it, Willie, you're an odd-looking person. You have the face of George Washington and the hair of Mary Todd Lincoln.

Anyway, I'm gonna keep this short, Willie, because I have to do the only thing that's more boring than your music—file my income tax return. But don't worry, you are always on my mind! Yee-ha!

A ROASTMASTER
MUST DANCE

*B*ACK IN THE DAY, COMEDIANS didn't just tell jokes. They sang, juggled, did card tricks and impressions, and even danced. In fact, Don Rickles still breaks out a little soft shoe during his headlining performances. To be a great Roastmaster, one must also be a multifaceted showman.

So when I was invited to compete on *Dancing with the Stars,* it was no surprise to my family that I agreed wholeheartedly. However, my comedy pals seemed rather shocked when they found out I was going to be a contestant. Drew Carey said, "Does that mean they have to change the name of the show?" Drew was merely pointing out that winners of the coveted mirror ball trophy are usually Olympic athletes or Super Bowl champs—not shlubby comics with a broken hip and high blood pressure. But I have the heart of a champion, even if the arteries are clogged.

I had even won a dance contest once at summer camp, by shaking my chubby eleven-year-old ass to Wild Cherry's classic, "Play That Funky Music, White Boy." Then, as a teenager mak-

BAR MITZVAH BOOGIE.

ing salads and fruit cups at the catering hall, I would occasionally take a break and peek into the ballroom through the little windows in the swinging kitchen doors and watch the well-dressed party guests attempt everything from the hora to the hustle. In college, I even went through a slam-dancing phase until my elbows swelled like grapefruits. Since then I've always been open to trying new styles. So now I figured, why not try ballroom dancing? I further reasoned that learning how to cha-cha-cha on national TV would be a fun way to pay homage to the multitalented Roastmasters who came before me. To regain the flexibility of my youth, I started taking classes at a local yoga studio. I loved going there every day. It reminded me of when I went to karate class as a kid. Barefoot. Solemn. Weirdly Asian. Ever since I earned my black belt at the age of ten, I've understood how much hard work it takes to master a physical art form. I was determined to take that knowledge and winning spirit with me onto the dance floor.

However, I soon discovered that my competition included Olympic gold medalists Misty May-Treanor and Maurice Green, Super Bowl champ Warren Sapp, Grammy-winning songstress Toni Braxton, soap opera diva Susan Lucci, Oscar-winning actress Cloris Leachman, celebrity chef Rocco DiSpirito, sex taper turned reality TV star Kim Kardashian, model turned mother of four Brooke Burke, and former boy bander turned even more gay Lance Bass. (Lance is a classy guy. He sent everybody in the cast a bag of Blow Pops on our first day.) In all, there were twelve other celebrities dancing with twelve professional ballroom dancers. That's one more couple than they usually have, making it the biggest season ever. The head bookmaker at the Wynn Casino in Vegas predicted me to finish dead last at 50–1. I figured being the underdog could only work in my favor.

On the first day of training, I showed up at the rehearsal studio and met my new dance partner, the infamous Polish princess of the ballroom Edyta Sliwinska. A world-class competitor, Edyta has been on the show every season, yet she has never won the trophy. In fact, she came in second the previous season and was a fan favorite to go all the way this coming season. At least, she was until she got teamed up with me.

I presented her with a bouquet of flowers as an advance thank-you for all the patience she would need in order to teach me her skills. As she took the bouquet, I couldn't help but notice her sharp blue eyes and even sharper fingernails. Her long legs, high spiky heels, and vampire-like accent made her seem almost menacing. I was definitely a little afraid of her.

Apparently she felt the same way because she mentioned my reputation as an insult comic and said she feared I would spend too much time making fun of her instead of learning my steps. I explained that even though I may think in punch lines, my dancing would be serious. In fact, if there were going to be any major distractions it would surely be her fault because she was impossible to look at without getting weak in my already shaky left hip. Very embarrassingly, I had broken my femur ice-skating with my nephews a few years earlier. Now it's held together with three titanium pins.

Excuses aside, I decided to approach my rehearsals like a Method actor. When I looked at Edyta I would try not to see her as the perfect beauty she is, but as my high school football coach Mr. Senese, who looked like a by-product of a rhino fucking a meatball. Ballroom dancing is physically demanding and the routines are complicated. I needed to concentrate if I was going to win.

As the rigorous daily training began, my feet ached constantly from the two-inch Cuban heels I was required to wear. I also had a persistent headache from trying to remember my complicated routines, not to mention the fact that the three pins holding my hip together felt like they might snap each time I landed on my left side. However, I was quite thrilled when the producers informed us that the first song chosen for us to dance to was my summer camp anthem, "Play That Funky Music, White Boy."

Still, my poor partner was faced with a near impossible job. She had to choreograph a cha-cha-cha routine that I could handle, then teach it to me, and then perform it with me on national television. And then do it all over again with the quickstep. That's right, she had to teach me two separate styles of dance in time for the show's big premiere. On top of that, she had to accomplish all this around my existing stand-up schedule. After a long Labor Day weekend of learning lock steps and spot turns in a midtown Manhattan dance studio, I remember telling Edyta that it was this level of commitment that would put us in the finals. She just smiled and continued filing her fingernails.

After rehearsal we would eat and have fun—falafel and borscht at the Comedy Cellar in Greenwich Village, knishes and cheesecake at the Carnegie Deli, hot dogs and beer at the New York Giants opening game. The running gag in the tabloids was that we would be the first couple ever to gain weight while training for a dance competition.

All of my East Coast friends were impressed with Edyta's appetite as well as her charm. She spoke several languages and made everybody she met feel special, including me. Above all, Edyta was transforming me into a dancer. She even incorporated a few of my funky summer camp moves into our routine. Each rehearsal I felt a little less like Fred Flintstone and a bit more like Fred Astaire. Before I knew it I had lost fifteen pounds and my ankles stopped hurting. My body was clearly going through some sort of ballroom puberty, and Edyta and I were becoming a good team—Eastern Europe meets North Jersey. I was more determined than ever to become the people's cha-cha-champion.

I asked my sister, aunt, uncle, and cousins to come to L.A. and be my cheering section. My aunt Donna and my uncle Joe have been dancing together for thirty years and I knew they would give me lots of love and inspiration. The night before the show we all went out for Chinese food. (Surely I was the only contestant eating barbecued spareribs that night.)

I was very nervous and my sister, Robyn, tried to put it all in perspective, "I keep bragging to everybody that my brother is going to be on *Dancing with the Stars*—as a star! So it doesn't matter how you do. It's really cool that they asked you to be on." Aunt Donna jumped in, "Nobody expects you to be good—just go out there and have fun." Uncle Joe advised, "Look confident, and no matter what happens just keep going." My cousin Enrique said, "Can you please introduce me to Lance Bass?"

The morning of the premiere I popped out of bed before my alarm went off, feeling like a kid on the opening day of Little League. I couldn't wait to suit up. My once painful dance shoes now felt like comfy slippers. Comedian pals from all over called to offer their support, including Chris Rock, who said "Fuck the dancing and start thinking of some *jokes*."

He reminded me that comedians rarely get a chance to be funny on prime-time television and that I should make the most of the moment. He said, "I had to host the fucking Oscars in order to get an opportunity like you're getting." Suddenly I felt obligated to dance well *and* get laughs on behalf of comics everywhere.

As I walked onto the set for the first time, I was greeted by all the same cameramen that I work with at the Comedy Central roasts every year. Everybody seemed to be rooting for me and our final rehearsal went almost perfectly. Every step of our cha-cha-cha felt crisp and the orchestra was playing that funky music to the max.

The only glitch happened halfway through when I got bopped hard on the nose with one of Edyta's hair curlers. I instinctively took my uncle's advice and just kept on dancing. As we sat down to change our shoes, the stage manager came over and asked us to do the routine one more time. Since the show would be live that night the director in the control room just wanted to make sure he had locked in all the best camera angles. After all, this was the top show on the number one network and everything had to be perfect. I took a swig of coffee and headed back to my mark.

The music started and I just felt it. Edyta and I were in a zone. I wasn't just remembering my steps . . . I was dancing. And it felt good. We were warmed up. We were ready. We were having fun out there.

Then as the orchestra approached the last bars, I dropped to my knee for my final move as I'd done a hundred times before. But as Edyta stepped past for her final kick around my back, she swung her hand toward my head and accidentally slashed me in my left eye with her long pointy fingernail. I felt a sting but ignored it as we made our final move, which involved Edyta kicking me in the back and pushing me to the floor in a mock fight. Then I stayed like that. Facedown on the dance floor. Just squirming on the ground holding my eye and moaning. The crew applauded. They thought it was part of the act. But I was afraid to get up. I was afraid to let go of my eye. I thought I might be holding it in place. The pain was awful. But I got up, walked off the dance floor, and sat down on a bench outside.

I still couldn't see. My eye hurt too much to even open it. Finally, an on-set emergency worker numbed it so I could relax. I pulled my eyelid open ever so slightly. My vision was extremely

FUCK!

blurry, but I could make out Edyta's worried face standing over me. I knew she felt bad. I tried to hold my eye open with my finger, but the sunlight quickly intensified the pain. After another ten minutes of denial, I finally agreed to go to an emergency room. Edyta went off to get a manicure.

Dr. Frankel at Cedars-Sinai told me I had a scratched cornea. I couldn't believe it. The VERY last move of the VERY last rehearsal and I scratch my cornea? Fuck! He gave me a tetanus shot and told me if I rested my eye I'd be fine in two or three days. He offered to prescribe some Vicodin and suggested I go home and crash.

My voice crackled. "But, Doc—I'm supposed to dance tonight. I've been practicing all summer. C'mon, Doc—what can you do?" He didn't answer. I just stared at him with my one good eye. Finally I said, "Say it ain't so, Doc." He looked at me and said, "Let me go make a phone call," and he disappeared for about forty-five minutes. Oy vey. This was torture. Who could he be calling? The cornea fairy? I was completely fucked and I knew it. I sat there boiling. Mad at the world. Mad at myself for even caring about this stupid show.

Eventually, Dr. Frankel gave me the name of an ophthalmologist in Beverly Hills who had agreed to see me right away. I jumped in the back of a production assistant's dirty red Buick and sped off to Beverly Hills in search of a miracle. After an intense examination, Dr. Hopp explained that even if he numbed the eye enough for me to open it, my vision would still be blurry and my eye would be extremely sensitive to light. He said that not only shouldn't I dance but that I probably *couldn't* dance under those bright TV lights even if I tried.

I said, "Doc, with all due respect. I'm dancing tonight. Will you help me?" He took a deep breath, shook his head in bewilderment, and laid out a bunch of scary eye tools. He put my head in a harness with a microscope on it, and he carefully placed a medicated contact lens over my cornea, which he said would act as an invisible Band-Aid to protect it. Then he placed a quarter of a millimeter size synthetic cork in my tear socket, and pulled a tiny unmarked eyedrop dispenser out of his desk drawer and said, "Put just one drop of this stuff in your eye right before you dance. It'll numb the pain for a few minutes. But don't do it more than once because it slows down your healing."

I said, "What's in it?"

He whispered, "You don't wanna know." Then he looked into my good eye and said, "Break a leg."

I said, "Thanks, Doc—I intend to."

When I finally got back to the studio, Edyta and all the producers were eagerly waiting for a report on my condition. I said, "Scratched cornea. Two doctors told me not to dance." The producers agreed that I shouldn't dance and risk hurting it further or accidentally launching my beloved partner into the orchestra pit. They recommended that we run the rehearsal footage from that morning and allow the judges to critique us based on that. They reasoned that this would get us the sympathy vote and make *Dancing with the Stars* history as the first couple ever to be judged on an injury-making performance. They said that if I rested tonight I'd probably be in better shape to make a triumphant return tomorrow night when we'd get to dance our fancy quickstep.

But I was in no mind to sit the night out (or make decisions). We had poured our hearts into this routine only to get injured on the last move of the last rehearsal. Edyta said that if I could walk

I should dance, but left the final decision up to me. I said, "The show must go on, right?" Edyta nodded in agreement. Conrad, the executive producer, said, "That's ridiculous! There are twelve other couples. The show goes on even if you don't dance. You'll just dance your second routine tomorrow. Unless of course you get eliminated after tonight's voting."

This was a big decision. Do I do the courageous thing or the strategic thing? Do I attempt the one-eyed, one-hipped cha-cha-cha in front of twenty-five million people, or do I play the rehearsal tape and hope for the sympathy vote to slide my way into the next round? Finally I said, "Fuck it. We're dancing! I was born to dance. And I'll die dancing if I have to." And then like a complete idiot, I donned a rhinestone eye patch and put on my two-inch Cuban heels, a pair of high-waisted Latin pants, and matching blue silk blouse, which all made me look like some sort of bisexual buccaneer of the ballroom.

Finally, the live broadcast began. Talk about pressure. Everyone I ever met or perhaps will meet was watching. Normally, I'm the guy backstage keeping it loose by cracking jokes and giving pep talks to the other performers. But this time I was sitting alone in a dark corner futilely attempting to administer my superpowered eyedrops. Eventually, the versatile actor and all-around nice guy Ted McGinley came over and did it for me. Ted is famous for appearing on shows right before they get canceled. But in that moment I didn't consider him the kiss of death, I considered him a saint for helping me see.

The celebrities were dancing quite well, but the judges were still giving lower than normal scores along with their usual cranky critiques. They told soap opera superstar Susan Lucci to gain weight. They told bootylicious reality star Kim Kardashian that

she had no spunk to go with the junk in her trunk. They told Olympic beach volleyball champ Misty May-Treanor that she did the tango like she had sand in her crotch.

Competing right before me was the show's oldest contestant ever, eighty-two-year-old Oscar-winning actress Cloris Leachman, who is madly in love with me. This crazy old GILF (Grandma I'd like to fox-trot) has had hot flashes for me ever since I met her at the roast for Bob Saget, where I said she was so old that "Shakespeare did *her* in the park." When I saw her a short time later at a cast party she pushed somebody out of the way and laid her head down on my lap and said, "I love you, Jeff. Do you love me?" Not wanting to hurt her feelings I said, "Yes, Cloris, I love you too." Then she nonchalantly placed my hand on her breast and squeezed it for a full ten seconds and moaned loudly. I was in too much shock and awe to pull my hand away. Then she said, "So, Jeffy darling, what do you think my first scores from the three judges will be?" I said, "I dunno, Cloris . . . 9-1-1?" She laughed so hard she peed herself more than usual.

Anyway, that night her fox-trot was a train wreck and her wig nearly fell off every time her partner dipped her. Plus, I think she was wearing the same gown she wore to the People's Choice Awards in '73. Regardless, the studio audience instantly fell in love with this crazy old broad. The place went wild when she put her leg up on the judge's table in a Hail Mary attempt to seduce them. Judges Carrie Anne, Bruno, and Len played along as she rambled incoherently for another ten minutes before giving her a lousy score of three fives out of possible tens.

Then it was my turn. Edyta gently removed my eye patch and placed it in my pocket. I took my mark. I wasn't nervous because I was numb. The funky music started and I soon began flailing

my arms and stumbling around the dance floor like an epileptic on fire. I was trying my hardest but it was no use. I was half blind, totally disoriented, and completely terrible. By the time I was done dancing my cha-cha-cha, any viewers tuning in late must have tried to pledge money to a charity telethon for the uncoordinated.

My critique by the judges was as painful as my wound. They

told me that despite my scratched cornea, I had no "musicality" and "wasn't cut out for the ballroom." Instead of acting like I cared, I just took Chris Rock's advice and landed a few zingers aimed mostly at the stuffy British judge Len Goodman, who, I said, "is so old he was originally a judge on *Walking Upright with the Stars.*" Bruno, the flamboyant Italian judge, told me that I would need to do something drastic in order to remain in the competition, so I ran over to him and threw my leg up on the table à la Cloris Leachman. That got me no extra points either. The judges gave me three fours, for a grand total of twelve points out of a possible thirty.

I laughed it off for the cameras, but inside I just couldn't believe it. Neither could host Tom Bergeron, who said, "I forgot we even had fours!" In fact, I had received the lowest score since a previous season when Heather Mills's prosthetic leg flew off midmambo and nearly gave a contusion to a cameraman. In the end, I just threw my arms up in exasperation and exclaimed, "Speaking of ballroom, these pants are kind of tight" and waddled offstage.

I was totally devastated. Not because I got such a low score, but because I couldn't believe how much I was falling in love with this ridiculous dance contest. I went home and ate seven slices of pizza. As I chomped the final hunk of crust, my girlfriend, Megan, told me that the judges were wrong and that she still thought I was gonna come back big and win the whole thing. I no longer believed her. I went to sleep dejected and in pain. Maybe it was the painkillers mixing with the pepperoni, but that night I had a wet dream about banging Cloris Leachman on the judges' table.

When I woke up the next morning my eye was stuck shut and my head was pounding. I went to see Dr. Hopp and by the time I left his office, my eye was beginning to open. In fact, he told me that the eyeball is the fastest-healing part of the body and that I should be okay to dance that night.

Now the pressure was really on. A record prime-time audience had watched my previous night's debacle. Tonight was my chance for a comeback. I was feeling very positive as my limo cruised through those studio gates.

As I got dressed, I went over our quickstep routine in my head. Our song was "I Get a Kick out of You," made popular by Jersey hero Frank Sinatra. With the words "I get no kick from champagne . . ." I would take a final swig from a flute of bubbly before kicking it off to the side. Then I would lock step over to Edyta in my tux and tails (wearing Buddy Hackett's gold cuff links for good luck), and present her with a bouquet of white roses. She'd take them, smell them, and dance into my arms, and off we'd go hopping, skipping, and jumping in circles around the floor like two actors in an old-time movie. The song ends as we dance side by side and launch into an impressive front snap kick, roundhouse kick, and spinning back kick into a flying double front snap kick finale. On the last note, I land on one knee as Edyta falls into my arms. The whole routine made me feel quite debonair—and when you throw in the custom rhinestone eye patch I was *fucking unstoppable*.

As I was tying my ascot, I got a text message from Cousin Sal, a friend who writes for his cousin's talk show, *Jimmy Kimmel Live*. Sal and I have been friends for many years—perhaps too many. I went to his wedding. I know his family. I even dated his sister.

However, when Sal and I were both writers at *The Man Show,* he would constantly find new ways to torture and abuse me every single fuckin' day, much to Jimmy's sheer delight. Sure, Sal pushed me into the pool during Adam Carolla's wedding and once spray-painted my punch lines onto the hood of my Porsche, but through all this we have somehow managed to stay buddies.

Anyway, Sal's text message said, "You're safe." I quickly texted him back, "Are you sure?" He immediately texted back, "Yes. Don't tell anybody." He knew that *I* knew that whoever gets voted off *Dancing with the Stars* automatically gets driven directly to *Jimmy Kimmel Live* to be interviewed about it on that night's broadcast. Sal also knew that I suspected that inside info occasionally gets leaked to members of Jimmy's staff so he can prepare for the segment.

This was incredible news. It meant Edyta and I would get to dance our incredible quickstep routine. She wasn't convinced when I told her. I totally was.

The live elimination began. My family was seated in the second row, wearing matching eye patches in solidarity.

Edyta and I stood there restlessly as one by one the other couples found out they were safe and performed their routines.

Near the end of the two-hour elimination, it was down to just me and Kim Kardashian. As we waited out the commercial break, Edyta dug her fingernails into my palms. I told her not to worry. "It's okay, Coach. My friend said we're safe. We're dancing next. Get ready. Stay loose." Then I waved to my family and began to stretch my hamstrings.

Our producer Rob came out and explained to me and Kim Kardashian that whichever of us got eliminated would have a chance to speak to the audience one last time. I asked him why he was looking at me and not Kim. Rob was surprised that I picked up on this and got strangely defensive. I took this as a very bad sign. A minute later we came back from commercial and Tom Bergeron said, "The couple with the lowest combined total and therefore leaving after only one dance is . . ." Dramatic music . . . scary lights . . . very long pause . . . "Jeff and Edyta."

My jaw dropped. I had trained every day for five weeks and I wasn't even going to dance the second routine. I just stood there in shock as Kim Kardashian danced her mambo. I simply couldn't swallow the fact that I'd stood onstage for two hours wearing this ridiculous outfit and I didn't even get to dance. As the show ended, I found myself embraced by the entire cast, who were now all wearing eye patches.

I tried to be a good sport, but when cohost Samantha Harris put a microphone in my face and asked me how I was feeling in that moment, I told the entire country the truth. I said, "This is a nightmare." Everybody laughed. As my good eye filled with tears I somehow remembered Chris Rock's advice and reluctantly admitted that even though I had tried hard, my dancing was probably more "ha-ha-ha than cha-cha-cha."

My phone started buzzing with condolences. My thirteen-year-old nephew Mitchell called and said, "Jeez, Uncle Jeff, that was harsh," and handed the phone to his eight-year-old brother Jared, who just cried. Then I got a text from Cousin Sal that said, "Sorry, dude—I messed up." Turns out that he was screwing with me the whole time. The bookies in Vegas were right, too. I had a better chance of winning the Westminster Dog Show than a dance competition. Worst of all, I had a Friars Club roast coming up in New York and I knew I was going to get absolutely clobbered over this.

So did I do the right thing by dancing with one eye? Many think I did. Jimmy Kimmel called me a hero for defying doctor's orders. Sportscaster Rich Eisen compared me to football legend Ronnie Lott, who had the tip of his finger cut off rather than miss a game. Judge Carrie Ann Inaba told me that my decision to dance that night will be remembered longer than if I had stayed in the competition another couple of weeks. My agent Heidi told me she was proud of me for handling myself like a "true pro." Whatever.

In private, I entered a post-dance depression. Not because I really cared about the stupid competition, but because I so wanted to keep on dancing with Edyta. Dancing with her was like playing tennis with Anna Kournikova or smoking crack with Amy Winehouse. It was a once-in-a-lifetime opportunity and it was now over just . . . like . . . that. People still stop me on the street and tell me I didn't get a fair shake. They tell me the judges should've given me a better score considering I was dancing with one eye (and two left feet). They tell me that crazy ol' Cloris used up all my airtime and the judges' goodwill. And of course, they tell me I'm a fool for believing that pathological prankster Cousin Sal when he told me I was "safe." But I always tell people not to feel bad for me because I got a lot out of the experience. For instance, I got this story—and a Roastmaster lives and dies by his stories.

ROASTING WITH THE STARS

Although my vision has never been the same, I can look back and see *Dancing with the Stars* as a positive experience. The producers invited me back for the season finale, where I not only got to perform my quickstep in front of twenty-three million people but I also got to have the last laugh by roasting the three finalists shortly before their last dance. Below is a play-by-play of the most-watched roasting in history.

"Hey, everybody! Remember me? I made *Dancing with the Stars* history . . . I came in thirteenth—on a show that normally has twelve contestants. I got injured before it was cool. [A reference to the injury-plagued season.] And people keep asking me if I lost weight. I say, 'I dunno, how much does my dignity weigh?'

"Do you know how embarrassing it was to get eliminated before an eighty-two-year-old? C'mon, Cloris, was that even dancing? Your partner Corky just dragged your lifeless body around the dance floor . . . that was like *Weekend at Bernie's: The Musical.* [Cloris started to come toward me.] Okay, Cloris, take it easy—you had your fifteen decades of fame.

"Because tonight it's all about these amazing finalists . . . Brooke Burke—with the perfect scores. Lance Bass—with the perfect hair. Warren Sapp—with the perfect boobs." Note: Warren didn't laugh at this at all. He just leered at me like he was going to eat me. I quickly changed direction.

"And folks, doesn't Brooke Burke look great tonight? Especially considering she just gave birth to her fifteenth kid backstage just three hours ago!

"And congratulations—I hear Lance is the father. Maybe the baby'll come out of the womb and the closet in the same day.

"But folks, what can you really say about Lance Bass that hasn't already been said about Clay Aiken? You know I love you, Lance—which Spice Girl were you again?" Lance was a great sport and answered, "Scary Spice!" Finally, I turned my attention to the three-hundred-pound elephant in the room. "And there he is . . . my friend, football legend, Warren Sapp . . . You're an inspiration, Warren. How do you dance eight hours a day every day for two months and stay so out of shape?" He finally cracked a smile—and a big one at that. "I used to think you were on steroids—then I realized you're just fat.

"But before I get my other eye poked out . . . I just want to say to the three of you, have fun out there, and remember: compared to me, you're all winners. Good night and good dancing!"

With that I got a standing ovation in front of the nation. I was euphoric. No entertainer had performed a roast in prime time since Dean Martin. It was a flawless performance that I'll never forget.

A SIMPLE THREE-STEP GUIDE TO FREEING YOUR INNER ROASTMASTER

FREEING YOUR INNER ROASTMASTER IS a difficult but vital part of the roasting experience. When you first try to get in touch with it, it will probably tell you to fuck off. There are, however, tricks for making the process easier. Here is a simple three-step exercise designed to help you unleash the beast within.

1. VISUALIZE YOUR INNER DAIS

In order to achieve true Roastmastery, it is important that you feel completely comfortable in the traditional roast environment. To do this, you must make roasting your own by visualizing your inner dais. Your inner dais is not confined by the laws of time and space the way a real dais is. Your inner dais can be long enough to accommodate the entire Pittsburgh Steelers starting line-up (if you hate that team) or small enough to hold only your parents (if you blame most of your problems on them).

Other ideas for imaginary dais members include childhood bullies, cheating exes, and monstrous dictators from history. In the case of hypothetical roast victims, it is not necessary for you to love those whom you insult. This is an exercise to get you feeling fearless and ferocious, so anyone you think will inspire vitriol and loosen your inhibitions should be invited to your inner roast. Just make sure you don't piss off your former flame so much that she goes down on Pol Pot.

2. PICTURE YOUR PERSONAL PODIUM

Your personal podium is the horse on which your inner Roast-master rides to glory. You can deck it out any way you like. It can be covered in Metallica stickers or festooned with Peruvian lilies, or it can be made of solid platinum with Cadillac fins jutting out from the sides, or perhaps one that is stocked to the gills with whiskey and cupcakes. (Your secret's out, Artie Lange!) The important thing is that you construct it according to the dreams and desires of your inner Roastmaster. Personally, I would love a podium that goes up in flames at the end of my show like Jimi Hendrix's guitar.

Now it is your turn. You must ask your inner Roastmaster what is necessary to make your perfect podium of power. Your inner Roastmaster is naked without it. It's okay for your inner Roastmaster to be naked, but only at the inner after-party.

3. LET LOOSE

Now that you've got a dais full of detestable scum and a levitating podium that folds out into a futon, it's time to go crazy. You don't have to worry about being clever, just cut deep and don't hold back. In fact, the next time you're bored at a party you may even want to try speed-roasting people in your head as they walk through the door. . . . "Excuse me, miss, you look familiar. Did you play a hooker on *Battlestar Galactica*?"

"Sir, congratulations on winning the banjo player from *Deliverance* look-alike contest!"

"Seriously, dude, thanks for breaking out your good camouflage shorts for the occasion. Who dressed you, FEMA? All kidding aside, what did you used to do for a living?"

If you need to drink a few martinis before you begin, that's fine. Just make sure your inner Roastmaster doesn't vomit on your outer shoes.

A ROASTMASTER IS NEVER SAFE AND NO ONE IS EVER SAFE FROM THE ROASTMASTER

AFTER JIMMY KIMMEL'S COUSIN SAL pranked me on *Dancing with the Stars*, we didn't talk for months. In his alleged heart, Sal believed that embarrassing me on national television was the greatest achievement of his low life. Sal even went on the radio and declared that he wasn't the least bit sorry for hurting my feelings and that he would do it one hundred times over because it was SO funny. He and Jimmy both told me I wasn't being a good sport, which, of course, is the worst insult you can say to an insult comic. So how could a guy who says such mean things not be able to take a joke? The answer is simple: A Roastmaster breaks balls—he doesn't crush dreams.

Being swept up in the excitement and romance of a ballroom dance competition, I just wasn't in the mood for Sal's crap. The truth is I can appreciate sick, sociopathic pranks—I hang out with Johnny Knoxville and the *Jackass* crew, for crying out loud. But Cousin Sal has no boundaries or conscience. He would prank his own mother if he thought it would make his cousin Jimmy laugh.

Roastmasters have feelings too. That's why we try to embolden one another at crucial moments. Take fellow Roastmaster Gilbert Gottfried. At The Comedy Central Roast of Bob Saget, he was about to go on after everybody killed. During the final commercial break, I looked over and saw Gilbert nervously fidgeting in his chair. I got up, sat down next to him, and whispered in his ear that he was *the man*. That this was *his* crowd. That he was gonna *destroy*. That he was gonna get up there and show everybody that he was the funniest guy in the room. Moments later he got up and roasted the roof off the place. Gilbert probably would have killed without the pep talk, but as a friend, I tried to do my small part.

So clearly Sal and I have fundamentally different philosophies regarding what is funny. I prefer it when everybody is in on the joke. If a friend breaks a leg, I may tease him about it to make him laugh. That's what a Roastmaster does. Sal is different. Sal will pour water on the floor hoping somebody breaks a leg just so he can videotape it and play it on the show.

For a while there it looked like Sal and I were never going to be friends again. I'd certainly been mad at Sal before—like the time he put milk in a water gun and sprayed my office wall at *The Man Show* and watched me go nuts for a week trying to figure out what the fuck died beneath my desk, or the week I was guest-cohosting *Jimmy Kimmel Live* and Sal barged into my dressing room three nights in a row and knocked my steak dinner on the floor for no reason at all. But this time there was no détente in sight. Sal and I had basically written each other off.

For almost two months, I didn't even go up to Jimmy's house on Sundays like I normally would. Watching football with the alumni from *The Man Show* writing staff is a long-standing tradition and it was painful for me to stay away. The truth is I missed everybody.

Finally, I couldn't take it anymore. I wasn't gonna let that chubby little troll keep me away from my friends and Jimmy's home cooking. So I went. And for moral support, I brought along

the fine actor and Roastmaster-in-training, John Stamos. We had become close when Comedy Central honored our mutual best pal Bob Saget and I helped Stamos prepare for his Roastmastering debut. Besides being painfully funny and annoyingly handsome, John was one of the finest rookie roasters I'd ever seen. His years of training in Broadway's best musicals and TV's worst sitcoms gave him the swagger to deliver daggers at his former co-star such as, "I was with you for 192 episodes of *Full House* and I can honestly say you don't have a funny bone in your body . . . unless of course you count the one time you sat on Dave Coulier's cock. And by 'sat on' I mean hungrily backed into. And by 'one time' I mean for eight seasons."

I was nervous as I climbed up the long walkway leading to Jimmy's house. Stamos told me to relax and reminded me that "these guys are your friends."

"Except Sal," I said.

"Well, we'll just see about that," Stamos said as he rang the doorbell. After all, "How hard could it be for Sal to apologize?" he added.

"Sal has never apologized to anybody in his life," I reminded him.

When I walked into Jimmy's house, everybody clapped. All the guys were happy to see me—except the prankster himself, who just paced around nervously. He couldn't even look at me.

After an hour of male bonding and a second helping of Jimmy's mouthwatering brisket, I started to say my good-byes when Sal cornered me. "Jeff, I think you should apologize to me for staying mad so long." This got a big laugh from the dozen half-buzzed dudes in sweatpants, and then Jimmy quickly jumped in and started after me, too. I tried to explain the difference between insulting someone who volunteers to be roasted and pranking someone on national television when he's at his most vulnerable, but my logic fell on deaf ears and thick skulls. After about half an hour I gave up and left.

A few weeks went by without any word from Sal. And then one day my doorbell rang and an unseen messenger dropped off a mysterious package from him. To make sure it wasn't anthrax or worse yet, one of Sal's infamous farts in a box, I had my housekeeper Matilda open it simply because she is braver than I am. Inside were four of the finest cigars from Cigars.com. Sweet! I checked the packing slip and it said there should be a note in the box. I found nothing. I immediately emailed Sal. "Was there supposed to be a note?"

He quickly wrote back, "No—do you need a note too?!" Jeez. I couldn't believe Sal was being a dick even when he was attempting not to be a dick. I wrote back that I needed "nothing from him." I broke one of the cigars in half and emailed him a picture of it as a symbol of our ruptured relationship. My message said, "Cigars.com? Next time try Apologies.com. Triumph the Insult Comic Dog smokes better cigars—and he's a puppet just like you." At this point I considered my friendship with Cousin Sal a thing of the past. Besides, I still had a long career ahead of me, none of which I owed to any of my cousins.

I went on the road to do stand-up. In Indianapolis a guy in the crowd yelled, "Fuck Sal!" It happened again in Vegas. Then again in New York. Over Thanksgiving, I took my nephews to Disneyland and while waiting in line for It's a Small World, a woman repeatedly asked me why I didn't ". . . punch that Cousin Sal in his fat fuckin' face?" Clearly comedy fans all over the country were getting more and more curious and furious about this thing between me and Cousin Sal.

By the time I got back to L.A. it was December and despite some lingering resentment, I was feeling in the holiday spirit. Once again, Sunday rolled around and I went over to Jimmy's to watch the game and sample some of his scrumptious chicken Parmesan. Sal was there as usual, looking squirrelly and cowering behind his uncle Frank, but I just ignored him. I almost didn't recognize him at first. He looked thinner and had lost some hair. He also seemed fidgety and I noticed that his beloved Dallas Cowboys were winning that day, so I quickly deduced that I was what was making him all jumpy. I figured the longer I ignored Sal, the more I was torturing him. Clearly, this raging battle between us was bothering him too.

Then something very unexpected happened. Tom Cruise walked into the house. Yeah, that's right. Tom Fucking Cruise! No bodyguards in tow. Just his mom carrying a box of cupcakes. Apparently, he and Jimmy recently hit it off when they exchanged Christmas presents on *Jimmy Kimmel Live* earlier that week. They pulled off a great bit together in which Tom presented Jimmy with the keys to a fully loaded Cadillac. Feigning surprise—then utter embarrassment—Jimmy handed Tom his present: an elaborately wrapped tin of caramel-flavored popcorn. Then Tom casually invited himself over to Jimmy's to watch football, and lo and behold, here he was.

Suddenly Jimmy's uncle Frank grabbed me by the arm and dragged me across the kitchen. "Hey, Tom, do you know my favorite comedian Jeff Ross?" Tom shook my hand, looked me in the eye, and said, "I believe we spoke briefly at the Friars Club roast of Matt Lauer." Ok. I was so psyched he remembered me

because I have had an entirely new respect for him ever since he magically appeared on the dais that day and roasted the popular host of *The Today Show*.

The two of them had a world-famous on-air argument a year earlier in which Tom got pissed off during the interview and called the lovable Matt Lauer "glib." With a smile and a wink, Tom explained to the audience of 1,500 Friars that he and Matt Lauer were actually pals. So tight, in fact, that when he was about to make his infamous couch-jumping appearance on *The Oprah Winfrey Show*, it was Matt Lauer who encouraged him to play up his blossoming relationship with his now-wife Katie Holmes.

He said Matt advised him at the time, "Your love is inspiring, go crazy, people will love you for it!" Tom tore into the popular journalist for ten sizzling minutes before saying, "Lose my number, you glib putz," and walked out of the room to a standing O. Wiping tears from his eyes, Matt Lauer leaped up and said, "Hey, Tom, can you stay? We can get you a booster seat." And Roastmaster du Jour Al Roker chimed in with, "He can't—his spaceship is coming to pick him up." It was a classic roast moment—and the whole event had been elevated by Tom's surprise appearance.

Now here he was again. Sal snuggled up next to me and whispered, "How about we let Top Gun decide who's right and who's wrong?" I instinctively agreed. I figured who better to point out the differences between making fun of somebody to their face or pranking them behind their back than a guy with actual on-the-dais experience like fellow Roastmaster Tom Cruise?

After my all-time favorite actor and his mom had some time to sample Jimmy's cooking and toss a football around with a few good men, our dear friend Sarah Silverman stood up and announced that it was time for the long-awaited sit-down between me and Sal—and that Tom Cruise would be making final judgment. Everybody grabbed a drink and a cupcake and gathered in Jimmy's spacious living room. Tom seemed momentarily confused about what was happening. So Sarah carefully explained that Sal has a history of messing with people, but that he might have gone too far this time.

For reasons I'll never understand, Tom Cruise agreed to listen to both sides of the story and then offer his opinion. Still, I felt confident. Surely the man who had portrayed so many righteous lawyers would see the difference between saying something mean like I do at roasts and *doing* something mean like Sal did to me.

I knew things were about to get heated, so I respectfully asked Tom in advance if I could curse in front of his mother. He looked at his mom, thought about it for more than a few seconds, and said, "No." It was actually heartwarming to know that even the guy who wore a mask while banging random hot chicks in *Eyes Wide Shut* doesn't use naughty words in front of his mom.

After Sarah told him the whole story about how much *Dancing with the Stars* meant to me and how I'd been embarrassed in front of twenty-three million people, Tom Cruise asked me how much I had rehearsed. I told him six hours a day for five weeks. Jimmy jumped in and said that was bullshit because I'd spent half the time eating pastries and chitchatting with my dance partner, Edyta. Jimmy also told Tom that he thought I had a crush on Edyta and that was the real reason why I was heartbroken about getting eliminated so quickly.

Tom studied me thoughtfully before asking, "Was the whole experience good for you professionally?" I answered as honestly as I could. "Yeah, I'm selling more tickets on the road, but if I had lasted a little longer it would've been a game changer." Sal and I argued back and forth until Sarah broke in to ask Tom Cruise's mom for her take on the proceedings thus far.

The elegant Mrs. C. looked over at me and Sal and said in her slow Kentucky by way of Jersey accent, "Well, I think the two of you are acting like . . . little boys." Ouch! Who would have guessed that in a room full of comedians, Tom Cruise's mom would get the biggest laugh?

Judge Tom asked me if I thought Sal's prank was funny. I confessed that the night after it happened I woke up at four in the morning laughing about it. I explained that it was Sal's crappy behavior since then that irked me. I mentioned how he had recently called Adam Carolla's popular radio show and made a point of saying that he didn't care about hurting my feelings and that he would do the same prank over again a hundred more times. Sal cut me off and told me I was being a pussy. I said, "So what, Sal? Even if I am being a pussy—why wouldn't you just apologize? That's what friends do!"

Sal dodged the question and explained that he thought of me as a member of his family. "That's no way to treat family," I said, holding back tears. "On the day I scratched my cornea, my family sat in the studio audience and wore eye patches in solidarity. They didn't try to throw me off my game on live television." Sal questioned the fact that a guy who insults people for a living could be so sensitive.

I told him he was just jealous because there's no show called *Dancing with the Cousins of the Stars*.

An exasperated Sarah Silverman retook the floor in defense of the beloved Kimmel clan. "What we have to understand is that the words 'I'm sorry' are not in the Italian vocabulary. One time, Jimmy got in an argument with his daughter and when he realized he was wrong he didn't say, 'I'm sorry,' he just ran into her bathroom and put on all her makeup." Everybody cracked up at this image, including Jimmy, who seemed to be relishing every second of this prolonged and pathetic pow-wow.

Tom Cruise leaned forward and systematically broke it all

down. After some intense questioning he got me to admit that some of the resentment I was feeling might be misdirected. Tom deduced that I was probably as mad at myself as I was at Sal. Not just because I was naive enough to believe him when he told me I was safe, but because I had ignored one of my own rules of live performance.

Buddy Hackett once told me always to turn my cell phone off at least an hour before any big show. Buddy's reasoning was that a Roastmaster owes it to his audience to tune out unnecessary distractions before taking the stage. I only left my phone on this once because my family was attending the show and I wanted them to be able to find me beforehand. Still, if I had listened to Buddy's advice, Cousin Sal would never have been able to get to me in that moment. But none of that really mattered that much now. What mattered was that my entire reputation as a good sport was on the line.

I finally decided to put the debate in terms Tom Cruise could relate to. He's been nominated for an Oscar three times and has never won. So I likened Sal's prank to my texting him from backstage at the Oscars to tell him he'd won, and then taking the footage of his bewildered reaction to his loss and replaying it later for laughs during a comedy bit.

"Wow. That's fucked up," Tom Cruise said, as his mom slapped him on the knee for cussing.

Tom looked deep into my eyes for what seemed like ten minutes. Then finally he turned to Cousin Sal and declared, "Sal, you hurt Jeff's feelings. I think you should apologize."

Sal sat there looking simultaneously dumbstruck *and* starstruck. He had asked the great Tom Cruise for the truth, but he couldn't handle the truth. For the first time ever, the wise guy who had mercilessly messed with me and countless others was going to have to say those two and a half words he so dreaded.

They didn't come out of his mouth easily. He tried a few times to add qualifiers that started with, "Listen, dude—" The judge and jury booed—we all craved sincerity. Tom Cruise stood up and said, "No qualifiers, Sal. Just say it!"

In a quivering voice, Sal looked down at his feet and said, "I'm . . . sorry . . . Jeff."

"Sorry for what?" I asked.

Sal finally looked me in the eyes and said, "I'm sorry . . . for . . . hurting your feelings."

I immediately accepted his apology. Tom pushed us all together for an official shaking of the hands. This was truly a historic moment. Cousin Sal had just taken his first step toward becoming an actual human being.

Even though the apology was forced, I knew I needed to forgive my friend completely. Staying mad at a prankster for playing a trick would be like staying mad at a puppy for peeing on the carpet. There's no point—he just can't help himself.

On Christmas Eve, Jimmy and Sarah invited me over for a giant seafood feast. I brought a gift for Cousin Sal. It was a pair of salt and pepper shakers in the form of two men hugging. Sal was clearly touched and gave me a hug in front of his entire family and the holy spirits of comedy. All was forgiven.

That night as we finally smoked those cigars Sal had given me and gazed out at the Christmas sky, I thought not of Santa Claus or the Magi but of the late great Buddy Hackett, who once advised me also that a Roastmaster should never hold a grudge. "While you're holding a grudge," he explained, "the other guy is out dancing."

However, on occasion a Roastmaster shall seek his revenge. But don't worry, Sal, *you're safe*.

A ROASTMASTER MUST KNOW HOW TO PARTY

*T*HERE IS NO BETTER PLACE to develop new material than at a social gathering. Whenever or wherever people are in a celebratory mood, a Roastmaster will surely flourish.

I've been to spring break, Mardi Gras, and the Super Bowl, but I'd always heard that nothing can compare to the revelry of a presidential inauguration. Buddy Hackett once told me that attending John F. Kennedy's swearing-in was the most exciting weekend of his life—mainly because he got to watch the new president shtup Marilyn Monroe in the Lincoln Bedroom. For these reasons—and my insatiable desire to absorb as much life experience as possible—I decided to go to President Obama's inauguration.

My flight to D.C. was festive. Everyone seemed to be heading to town for the big event, including a few of the last remaining Tuskegee Airmen, the black fighter pilots whose service during World War II helped convince President Eisenhower to end racial segregation in the military. Now here they were flying to D.C. to watch a black man become commander-in-chief. I was kvelling. I have never seen so many flashy garment bags and fancy hatboxes on one aircraft. Clearly we were all determined to dress up and party down in honor of this promising new guy, the notorious B. H. O.

Since hotel rooms were scarce, I stayed with my college pal Eric and his family. (I call him Dosage for undisclosable reasons that go back to a party in his dorm room freshman year.) The day before the actual inauguration Obama called on all Americans to donate a day of service to the nation in honor of Martin Luther King's birthday. This inspired me, Dosage, and his wife, Karen, and their three kids, Adam, Jordan, and Ethan, to bundle up and head to RFK Stadium to help 12,000 other volunteers stuff care packages for the troops overseas.

After about twenty minutes, the kids got cold and started to whine. (Okay, maybe I was the one whining.) Regardless, despite the freezing temperatures it was heartwarming to be volunteering alongside so many of our fellow citizens, all working toward a common cause—even if it meant catching common colds. After writing a stack of thank-you letters to the soldiers, we were about to head out when I noticed a crowd forming in front of a small stage and a couple of camera crews setting up. Like a showbiz bug, I was drawn to the lights. I asked one of the reporters what they were here to cover. He said there was a rumor our new savior might be stopping by to say a few words to the volunteers. Within minutes, thousands of people stopped working and surrounded the stage. The event's organizers nervously stood at attention behind a microphone. I got goose bumps. We could feel his presence.

As we stood there I thought about what I might say if I got

the chance to shake Obama's hand. I decided I would tell him I wanted to host a comedy fund-raiser to build a basketball court on the South Lawn of the White House. President Nixon installed a bowling alley in the basement and President Clinton had a putting green created just outside the Oval Office, so why shouldn't Barack be able to break a sweat *his* way? Across the backboard it could say "The Audacity of Hoops."

Finally, the organizer of the event stepped up to the podium. The crowd roared. She nervously cleared her throat, thanked us all for coming, and began to introduce her very special guest . . . drumroll, please . . . local Channel 9 news anchor Bruce Johnson! Oh snap! Our chants of "Yes we can!" suddenly turned into "No she didn't!" and we took off in search of warmer pastures.

That night we went to a party honoring Sarah Silverman's influential campaign video in which she successfully hocked young Jews into schlepping down to Florida to convince their grandparents why they needed to vote for this brilliant schvartzer with the weird name. Even though the rapper Nelly also performed three songs the party was still really fun. Afterward, we went back to Sarah's hotel suite, got stoned, and ate too much pizza.

The next morning we got up before dawn and walked a mile to the subway. However, when we finally got downtown and saw the soldiers and the tanks and the mass of humanity trying to get through the security barricades, I quickly realized that this event wasn't going to be like anything else I'd ever experienced. I'd often heard Obama compared to a rock star. Forget it—this guy gives rock stars away on Halloween. No mere rock star could draw this diverse a crowd to an outdoor performance in ten-degree weather at eight o'clock in the morning. But here we were. All two million of us. Freezing our patriotic asses off.

As we waited in a jubilant mob of special blue ticket holders for hours, a Jamaican guy recognized me. "Hey, ain't you the guy who makes fun of all the big shots? Ain't you the Roastmaster General?" I offered up a big smile as he took a picture of me surrounded by all his buddies. Before long I was the center of attention. A middle-aged black lady yelled out, "Hey, it's cold out here—roast Barack!"

Now I was truly what we Roastmasters like to call on the fucking spot. My mind raced, thinking of ways to roast the untouchable Obama. Other than his floppy ears and his giant dick, what can you really make fun of before he's even taken office? But with nothing else to do except stand there and freeze, I decided to just start talking. "Okay, people, let's start with that middle name of his . . . which, of course, is . . . Hussein. That's right, his full name is Barack Hussein Obama. I mean, who am I—Jeff Hitler Ross? It sounds crazy, right? The leader of the free world shares a name with a sadistic dictator. Personally, I think he needs to take half a day off, go downtown, and change that shit. For forty bucks he could be Barack 'Big Dick' Obama. Then again, who knows, maybe he calls his balls Uday and Qusay."

I was on a roll and the wait time was starting to fly. "I hear Barack's penis is so big he refers to it as his *stimulus package*. I hear Barack's penis is so big it can beat him in basketball. I hear Barack's penis is so big today they're using it as a security barricade. Seriously, it's big! I hear Michelle calls it *Air Force Two*."

We finally made it through the metal detectors and onto the Mall just as the transfer of power was about to take place. Unfortunately, the only spot left to stand was behind a gigantic oak tree. I couldn't see a fucking thing, but I could clearly hear the booing coming from the front of the crowd as George W. Bush was introduced to the American public as their president for the very last time. If it hadn't been so cold, people probably would have been throwing their shoes at him too. In that moment, I actually felt sorry for the guy—almost as sorry as when I told Courtney Love she looked worse than Kurt Cobain.

Moments later, the newly elected leader of the free world finally emerged from the giant doors of the Capitol Building. To say the place went ape shit is an understatement. In the ruckus, I found a way to balance myself on the railing of a staircase so I'd be just high enough to see a portion of Obama's head on the JumboTron way across the lawn. He was smiling widely as he hugged his wife and daughters in front of the crowd. I was glad he finally looked so happy. Months earlier, on the night Obama was elected, I remember thinking how he was deprived of a real celebration because the grandmother who raised him had died the night before. Today, with all of us, he was finally enjoying the moment. This was his party. It was a Barack Mitzvah.

Standing just above me on the staircase was an elderly black woman from New Jersey named Francine. She was wearing a bright purple coat with a matching hat and carrying a fancy cane. She told me it was the happiest day of her life. I told her I was honored to be sharing it with her and offered her half of my granola bar. By the time Aretha Franklin sang the opening number, Francine and I were both crying. Not just because of the emotion of the performance, but because I had just told her my Aretha Franklin jokes from the Matt Lauer roast.

"I've never been to a show where the fat lady sings in the beginning. Instead of 'America the Beautiful,' she accidentally sang 'America the Delicious.' Forget R-E-S-P-E-C-T, Aretha Franklin never forgets a R-E-C-I-P-E."

Anyway, by the time Über-Pastor Rick Warren gave the benediction I could no longer feel my toes and I had to pee so badly I started to cry again. Then finally at the strike of noon the president-elect stepped up to center stage, raised his hand, and solemnly swore to uphold the Constitution of the United States of America. Except for a few flubbed words, it was official. A black man was in charge. Finally, teachers and parents won't just be waxing rhetorical when they tell kids that any one of them—no matter what they look like—can grow up and become president. It was a great moment. Francine and I high-fived.

As the newly minted President Obama stepped up to the microphone to deliver his highly anticipated inaugural address, a police officer came over and randomly made me, Francine, and a bunch of other people get off the staircase we'd been perched on the whole time. Now with nowhere left even to stand, Dosage and I began to retreat. Even though I couldn't really hear or see the actual speech, I was still glad I went. There was a warm feeling in the cold air.

That night Dosage and I put on tuxedos with long johns underneath and went to an inaugural ball hosted by the Creative Coalition, a bipartisan organization of artistic types who help protect free speech. As a citizen who occasionally says fucked-up shit in public, I feel an obligation to support their events and drink their booze.

I immediately cozied up to Spike Lee, who somehow managed to look cranky even while wearing a top hat. "Spike, you know the last president to wear a top hat to an inauguration was J. F. K. So you're reviving a great tradition," I told him. Spike seemed pleased with that notion, but still went right back to politely ignoring me.

I met another great director, Barry Levinson, who told me he saw the documentary I directed about performing in Iraq and that he enjoyed it very much. Wow. That was nice to hear. I also got to meet the fine actress Anne "Call me Annie" Hathaway, who laughed at all my jokes and told me about driving down with her friends to D.C. from Jersey just after graduating from high school to protest the Supreme Court's decision to award Bush the presidency over Al Gore. After hearing Sting, Elvis Costello, and blues legend Sam Moore sing together and making fast work of a couple of homemade creamsicles, I was hearing out the door when a paparazzo pointed to the commemorative button on my coat that depicted Obama in Gene Simmons KISS makeup, and asked if I was going to pick up any souvenirs before I left town. I said, "Nah, I already bought three buttons, two T-shirts, and a Senate seat."

Since much of the downtown area was blocked off to traffic, Dosage and I hired a pedicab to take us home. We laughed and smoked cigars as this open carriage carried us through the nation's capital like a couple of fancy gents. Suddenly we were back in the days of Lincoln. Now, I bet *he* had a fun inauguration . . .

"Hey, Abe, you having a good time? Well, tell your face. Seriously, are you hiding Harriet Tubman in your hat or are you just happy to see me?" I tipped my imaginary top hat to our founding Friar, Emmanuel J. Roastenberg—after all, a Roastmaster must continually pay homage to the greats who came before him.

A ROASTMASTER
NEEDS NO INTRODUCTION

*B*EFORE I WAS KNOWN AS the Roastmaster General Jeffrey Ross, I was always introduced onstage as *Jeffrey Lifschultz*, which is the name on my birth certificate. I know, I know—it's the worst show business name since Arnold Dolores Schwarzenegger. But I'm still proud of it and I'll never legally change it because I come from a long line of fine hardworking and respected Lifschultzes. Since I was only doing stand-up as a hobby to meet chicks, it didn't seem to matter that I had a stage name that could barely fit on a marquee. I figured as long as it was pronounced properly, I'd be fine. I even had a joke about it in my fledgling act, "My last name is Lifschultz. That's an old Hebrew word meaning, 'Hey, you oughta change that.' "

After years of performing at amateur nights and random hell gigs up and down the Eastern Seaboard, I finally landed a spot on *Star Search,* the popular afternoon TV talent show hosted by a semiretired Ed McMahon. Like millions of people, I first discovered Ed on *The Tonight Show,* where he was Johnny Carson's

Jeff
Lifschultz

buzzed and buoyant late-night sidekick. I was too young to get the jokes back then, but I remember my mom and dad laughing hard whenever Don Rickles was a guest because he would inevitably ignore Johnny and just rip on poor Ed for his alleged drinking. "Hey, Ed, burp already. I hope your beer truck crashes." Then Ed would just crack up uncontrollably—and it all made for good TV.

Over the years, Ed's day job on *Star Search* launched the careers of some talented comics, including Dennis Miller, Ray Romano, Richard Jeni, Rosie O'Donnell, and Sinbad. This was just the validation I had been waiting for. Even my uncle Murray watched *Star Search*. No doubt the entire Lifschultz clan would be tuning in and rooting for me. I was determined to stay long enough to win the $100,000 grand prize awarded by Ed McMahon at the end of the season. Clearly this show was my ticket to stardom. I was going to be the next Sinbad.

I was flown first-class for the first time down to Disney World in Orlando, where *Star Search* was taped. I brought along four duffel bags stuffed with every shirt, jacket, sock, belt, and boot I owned, figuring I'd need a new outfit for each round of the competition. With my energy weakened by the low-carb Nutra-System diet plan I had been on since the moment I found out I was going to be appearing on national TV for the very first time, I nearly got a triple hernia dragging my luggage into the hotel lobby. Luckily, my fellow New Jersey comedy pal Keith Robinson was checking out as I was checking in. I begged him to help me carry my bags through the rest of the cavernous lobby, past the enormous pool, across a vast lawn, and up the stairs into my tiny room. As we dragged the duffels, Keith told me the heartbreaking story of how his nine-episode *Star Search* winning streak was broken earlier that day when he was defeated by a comedian named John Bizarre by only "half a star." Hmm . . . would I be his next victim?

The next day I woke up more nervous than I'd been since my Bar Mitzvah. I weighed myself on the hotel room scale and was very proud to see that I had lost twenty-two pounds in two and a half months. I went over my jokes in my head one more time before arriving at the studio wearing a new gold silk western-style jacket from Filene's Basement—slimmed down, pumped up, and ready for my TV debut.

After all the dancers, singers, models, and kids competed in their respective categories, it was finally time for the comedians to face off. I was up first. As I waited in the wings for my introduction, all I could think about was urinating. I asked the stage manager if there was a men's room nearby. He said I didn't have time. I said, "I'm sorry but I can't go out there like this—" and I flung open a side stage door and ran out into the crowded theme park. With my zipper half undone, I frantically ran around Frontierland looking for a bathroom. No luck. I've always been a panic pisser and I was clearly in a state of preshow hysteria at this moment. I started to whip it out behind a churro stand when the stage manager grabbed my jacket and dragged me back into the studio just in time for Ed McMahon to introduce me to America . . . "Please welcome this week's comedy challenger . . . Jeffrey Lipshits!"

Lipshits? Huh? What? I haven't been called Lipshits since the seventh grade! The joke I'd heard a zillion times as a kid, "Hey, if your lip shits, then my ass talks," reverberated through my skull as I stumbled through my two-and-a-half-minute routine. Afterward I hobbled to a bathroom and let out a giant piss of relief.

Despite my bursting bladder and bungled intro, I scored three out of a possible four stars from the judges. Then I sat anxiously in the wings and watched my opponent, a lady comic from the Midwest whose name I have since forgotten. What I do remember is that halfway through her set she froze mid-sentence and just stood there like a deer in the stage lights. After about twenty excruciating seconds she awkwardly sauntered offstage to no applause at all. Ed McMahon lifted my hand in the air and proclaimed me the winner by a staggering two whole stars! Sadly, this was the greatest moment of my life.

This meant I got to stay for another round and take on the defending champion—the likable but rather unbizarre John Bizarre. This also meant I had to come up with a new outfit and fresh material. That night I went through my duffel bags and pulled out my best *Beverly Hills 90210* ensemble to match my Jason Priestley sideburns.

I also went through my notebooks and came up with another two and a half minutes of material that I thought would kill. But there were no comedy clubs around to try out my jokes, so I decided to get in a warm-up set on one of the small boats ferrying guests across a romantic lake to the restaurants over at Disney's Pleasure Island. I very politely introduced myself to the teenage captain and asked him if I could try out my jokes on the passengers. His voice cracked as he said, "Okay, but please don't make any jokes about Mickey Mouse."

"Don't worry, all my jokes are about Goofy humping Pluto."

Uncertain as to whether or not I was joking, the confused teenager reluctantly handed me his microphone. I cleared my throat, took a deep breath, and began. "Hey, everybody, my name is Jeffrey Lifschultz and I'm going to be competing on *Star Search* tomorrow and I was hoping to try out some of my material on you nice vacationers. . . ."

Only a few of the passengers clapped. It was at this point that I looked out and realized that nearly everyone on the boat was Japanese. I had no option but to continue. I launched into a tried-and-true bit I had about single life. "Anybody ever been on a blind date?" (No response.) "Well, I let my great-grandma Rosie fix me up on one recently. . . . I go to this chick's house . . . she opens the door . . . I took one look . . . heinous—that was her name, *Heinous*. You should see her sister, *Horrendous*. Her Hebrew name was *Yichhh*."

Nobody was laughing. Certainly not the bewildered Japanese tourists. Not even the ugly Canadian newlyweds. And especially not the captain, who looked so pissed I thought he might burst into puberty right on the spot and yell at me. Figuring this was all good practice for live television, I continued to plow through my routine as the Japanese people snapped my photo. Out of the ten or so bits I tried, maybe three got a response—and those were mostly yawns. Afterward, I sheepishly handed the microphone back to the captain, threw myself overboard, and swam back to the hotel.

The next day when Ed McMahon introduced me he fudged my name even worse than the previous time. "Please welcome our returning comedy challenger . . . Jeffrey Lacksticks!"

I just froze. *Lacksticks? Who the fuck is Lacksticks?*

Ed realized his mistake and tried again . . . "Remember this name, America, it's . . . Jeff—Lifzuilteiniz." Better than Lipshits, but still . . . Despite the botched intro, it was my inexperience and rookie material that made me lose (by a mere half star) to John Bizarre—a name I'll never forget.

On the long (coach) flight back to Newark Airport I had a moment of clarity: If I really wanted to be a professional stand-up comedian, either I was going to have to change my name for show business, or my family was going to have to change theirs to avoid national embarrassment.

So, in loving tribute to Great-Grandma Rosie Lifschultz, I decided to start using my middle name, which is Ross. After all, it was Great-Grandma Rosie who founded the catering hall where I first learned to make fun of people. By all accounts she was a class act with a rebellious tongue. I like to believe her spirit lives on through me.

Nowadays, thanks to confidence gained over two decades of experience, nothing rattles me. When a host or emcee says, "Mr. Ross, how would you like to be introduced?" I always say, "I don't care. Just make it your own." The truth is, it almost doesn't matter what comes directly before you. You must stay in the moment and go with whatever happens. A Roastmaster must create his own flow, his own mood. In the end, only your material matters.

As for Ed McMahon, I didn't run into him again until years later when I was performing on the annual Jerry Lewis Labor Day Telethon to raise money for kids with muscular dystrophy. Since I was personally invited to perform by Jerry Lewis, I felt confident enough to ask him to reintroduce me to Ed McMahon, who was cohosting the telethon with him. Backstage I told Ed how he had inspired me to change my professional name to Jeffrey Ross and I thanked him for guiding me to this first big step toward being an entertainer for life. Ed let out his trademark Santa Claus laugh, put his arm around me, and told me he was glad to be of service. Then he finished his drink, walked out onto the stage, and proceeded to introduce me as ". . . a hot young comic named Josh Ross!"

A ROASTMASTER MUST THINK BIG

*W*HEN I FIRST STARTED APPEARING at the annual Friars Club roasts, I was always the youngest guy on the dais. In fact, my standard opening line was, "Look at this place—I've seen younger faces on cash." Back then roasting was a lost art—like jousting or dragon slaying or journalism. All the young, hip, "alternative" comics downtown teased me because I loved to get all gussied up and bash the old guys uptown. They didn't see it as retro or cool, they just saw it as a waste of time. But to me, putting on a tuxedo and trading jabs with octogenarians was the definition of "alternative" comedy. Still, I worried about being pigeonholed.

Dave Chappelle gave me some great advice. "Every comic needs a lane," he said. "Something they're known for. Something they love and accept. Hopefully something that has endless possibilities." Since Dave's walked away from more money than most comedians ever make in their lives, I decided to heed his counsel and accept the popularity of the roasts I helped resurrect.

However, it wasn't until I was introduced on *Jimmy Kimmel Live* as "The Roastmaster General" that I felt fully anointed. Even at that point, though, I never could have imagined that my peculiar passion for put-downs and podiums would become so mainstream. But I'll never think small again. Especially since I was recently asked to do nothing less than help the president save the world with my unique expertise.

I was most of the way through my Friday late show at Zanies in Nashville. Kix Brooks from Brooks and Dunn was onstage with me. I had pulled him up out of the audience as if I didn't know who he was. Even though he wasn't wearing his cowboy hat, most of the "music city" crowd recognized him anyway. "What do you do, sir?" I asked. Kix deadpanned, "I'm one half of Brooks and Dunn." The crowd applauded. I shrugged and said, "What is that? An accounting firm?"

Suddenly Rose, the manager, ran up onstage with an urgent note. It said "Please call the White House." There was a phone number. "Damn you, Cousin Sal!" I screamed, thinking it must be another prank. But Rose was adamant. Kix sat down at the keyboard and sang "Red Dirt Road" while I ran backstage to make that call. Sure enough, within seconds I was being connected to the Commander in Chief.

"Yes, Mr. President."

"Is this the Roastmaster General?"

"No, it's Rush Limbaugh's hemorrhoid. What can I do for you, sir?"

"I'm sorry to interrupt your show, but I desperately need your help saving the environment."

"No shit?"

"Ya see, billionaires Bill Gates and George Soros have offered to leave their fortunes to the fight against global warming if you are willing to roast its greatest and fattest advocate, Al Gore, in front of the United Nations General Assembly tonight."

With confidence I take a deep breath and say, "Mr. President—it would be an honor. But can you throw in a few bucks for airfare?"

Of course, I pocketed the airfare and flew to New York atop my government-issued supersonic podium. However, due to laws restricting the airspace over Manhattan, I am forced to land in Yonkers and take a cab to the United Nations. Luckily, the Polish delegation was also late because they went to the International House of Pancakes on Ninth Avenue accidentally.

Upon arriving I was greeted by the annoying publicist of the secretary-general of the United Nations. After she told me how "thrilled everybody was that I could make it on such short notice," she got all up in my grill and proceeded to tell me, the Roastmaster General, not to tease Al Gore about his weight gain. I said, "Don't worry, all my fat jokes are about Tipper," and strutted out into the illustrious General Assembly beaming with confidence. After all, when you're an internationally-renowned insult comic on a mission from the president you have a license to kill.

When I walked out to the podium the crowd of diplomats went crazy. My appearance was a welcome departure from world matters. For openers, I took off my shoe like Khrushchev during his infamous 1960 UN address and banged it on the podium while yelling, "Al Gore, I will bury you!" The Russian ambassador Sergei Kislyak laughed so hard Stolichnaya came out of his nose. However, Al Gore himself did not seem amused. Turns out nobody had bothered to tell him I was coming.

Normally, I don't do surprise roasts. It's always best when the guest of honor has had time to prepare a rebuttal. But since this wasn't really a roast as much as a call to service—I decided it was okay this one time. Because of the immense respect I have for our former vice president and Nobel laureate, I put my hand on his shoulder and opened with a backhanded compliment:

"First off, I think we should all give Al Gore a big round of applause for the beautiful weather we had today! Don't you just love his plan to get so fat he blocks out the sun and prevents global warming? The crowd went berserk, I was already on a roll. . . .

"Seriously, what an honor it is to be here. The stakes couldn't be bigger and the guest of honor couldn't be fatter.

"You keep talking about the Greenhouse Effect—but what about the Waffle House effect?

Hey, Al—here's another 'Inconvenient Truth'—you're fucking fat!

"But seriously, congrats on the success of your documentary. I only saw the first ten minutes because the air-conditioning broke in the theater. No way I'm gonna watch a glacier-melt for two hours while I'm sweating my balls off.

"All kidding aside, Al—the people of the world need you—especially the ones who work at Burger King."

Usually, at this point I would say something nice and get off, but I was interrupted by the sound of a screaming gunman. Turns out a member of the Angolan delegation was attempting to assassinate my roastee because of his repeated denunciations of that country's decades-long abuses of its ecosystems. "God is great and Gore is fat!" the gunman shouted as a bullet came whizzing toward the front of the room.

Suddenly, I grabbed hold of my bulletproof podium and

leaped in front of Al Gore, saving his life. Not only did I spare the life of the beloved patriot but the bullet ricocheted off my podium and killed the Angolan terrorist and that annoying publicist. Did any of this make the newspapers? Of course not. Because exciting experiences like this happen every day in the life of a Roastmaster.

A ROASTMASTER SHOULD NEVER FEAR A TOUGH ROOM

*B*ECAUSE WE ROASTMASTERS ARE LUCKY enough to live in a country that allows us to say whatever we want, I feel we have a particular duty to use our powers for good. Therefore, every other gig I do is a freebie, which means that half the time I'm making fun of people, I am doing it out of the goodness of my heart. As the Roastmaster General of the United States of America, I implore all others to do the same.

However, working for free does have its challenges. It's easy to get laughs at a big show where people are drinking and having a good time. But what happens when you're donating your services to the poor and the sick and the lame? Benefits, telethons, fundraisers, I've bombed at all of them.

Consequently, I've learned a few tricks over the years. For instance, at a benefit for people with Crohn's disease, always go on before dinner. If working a fund-raiser for people with dyslexia, make sure they spell your name right on the invitations. Alzheimer's shows are the easiest because you can repeat your material.

Normally at these types of gigs, you are required to follow a depressing speech or video. One of my best pals is Bob Saget, who lost his sister Gay to scleroderma, a painful skin disease the exact cause of which is not known. Bob started the show by introducing a video he directed that chronicled the suffering of a disfigured teenager who couldn't walk, swallow, or breathe properly. The video ended and everyone in the crowd wiped away tears. Then Bob, who was visibly shaken, swallowed hard before introducing the comedy portion of the show, which was little old me. I didn't ignore the elephant in the room. Instead, I went right for it. "How about that video?" I began. "Man, I haven't seen anything that depressing since Bob Saget's HBO special."

This was merely the icebreaker. It took me another three minutes until the audience started to thaw. By the end of my twelve-minute performance, I felt like I'd single-handedly changed the direction of an iceberg.

It's not that I had a bag of tricks or a barrage of scleroderma jokes. It's just that I dug in and committed to changing the subject from disease to the fat guy in the front row, whose name coincidentally was Melvin Icenberg. "Nice to meet you, Melvin. Didn't I see you on *To Catch a Predator*—twice?"

On rare occasions, this "roasting the audience strategy" backfires. At a black-tie affair for Larry King's Cardiac Research Foundation, there was a priest sitting right in the front. I said, "Great to see you, Father. When did you get out?" Turns out the guy had recently been locked up for some dubious activities of an unseemly nature. People started hissing and booing and instead of moving an iceberg my act went down like the *Titanic*.

It took seven years for Larry King to forgive me. When he finally invited me on his CNN talk show to discuss politics just four days before the presidential elections, I pissed him off all over again when I said, "Larry, I just want to say it's an honor to be spending Halloween with the Cryptkeeper." Clearly, I have no self-control. Larry leered at me like I just snapped his suspenders.

Of course giving back feels good but it's also great roasting practice. Every Christmas Day, I try to spend at least a few hours feeding the homeless, who line up for a hot meal outside the Laugh Factory on Sunset Boulevard in Hollywood. As the son of a caterer, I especially feel a need to feed hungry people. Once everybody has had plenty of turkey, the show begins. The comics, often still wearing their aprons, hop onstage and attempt to enter-

tain an audience of lost souls as they settle into their tryptophan comas.

"What a crowd. What is this, a private party for the dregs of society?

"Sir, relax—what, is your shopping cart double-parked? Please . . . just sit back and take off one of your seven jackets.

"All kidding aside—sir, how is it possible to smell like shit *and* diarrhea? I've never done a show with a two-stink minimum.

"Anyway, that's my time! Merry Christmas, everybody! Don't forget to tip your Dumpster!"

My particular brand of tough love usually goes over big with this chatty but receptive crowd. After all, nobody is better at laughing at themselves and talking to themselves than homeless people. The general rule is: the poorer the crowd, the more they enjoy the show.

That's why I'm always reluctant to perform for the rich and hoity-toity. I once performed at a swanky affair for gun control that made me want to shoot somebody. The event was held in a gigantic tent on a sprawling estate in Beverly Hills. I put on my best tuxedo and got there an hour early to try to become one with my surroundings. I checked the staging, adjusted the lighting, and ate some shrimp.

As I admired the extravagant floral arrangements, the seventeen-piece orchestra, and the abundant trays of hors d'oeuvres, I began to realize that I was perhaps the least important component of the evening. After a seven-course meal, eight speeches, nine videos, and a piano recital from the host's ten-year-old daughter, the bandleader thanked everybody for coming and walked off the stage. Suddenly, the lady hosting the event ran up to the mic and said, "Oh yeah, there's just one more thing—please welcome . . . tonight's . . . comedian! Thanks for coming, every-body!" That was it—no name, no credits, no respect.

The overdressed and unimpressed audience grabbed their swag bags and began storming the valet. "What's your rush?" I said. "The valet parking here is a lot like gun control laws—there's a three-month waiting period."

Nothing.

"Wow, tough tent."

I proceeded to redefine bombing. I tried to maintain my composure as waiters noisily collected the dirty silverware off the tables. The rest of my set is blocked out of my head like a death in the family. All I remember is my voice cracking mid–punch line as I noticed one of my favorite comedy stars, Will Ferrell, get up and leave in the middle of my act.

Great, I thought. *I'm bombing so bad, the nicest guy in Holly-wood is walking out on me.* Funny or die indeed.

As painful as that gig was, there's no tougher room to per-form in than a hospital room. I've been invited by the USO to visit wounded soldiers a bunch of times and it always takes me days to recover emotionally. However, many of the wounded I've met there will never fully recover. I can tell you firsthand that not every patient becomes well enough to be interviewed for docu-mentaries or march in parades.

When you walk into an injured person's room you never know what to expect. Could be a blind guy holding his baby, could be a teenage marine eager to return to his buddies, could be a guy with a piece of his head missing who doesn't seem to know you're even there. In the saddest cases, I'm really just stopping by to break up the hours of monotony for the family members.

My basic strategy is to smile, walk in, and try not to stare.

Then I usually start crackin' jokes about how hot the nurses are or how bad the food is. "I just had breakfast downstairs, so don't be surprised if I'm lying next to you in a few minutes."

My goal is to manufacture smiles by adding insult to injuries. If a guy is really messed up and has limbs missing or metal pins coming out of his bones, I usually accuse him of faking the whole thing just to get out of jury duty.

Then I take a seat on the corner of the bed and ask what happened. Whether it's a marine who got shot in the face by a sniper or a Seabee who burned his legs laying asphalt, I've found that war heroes are eager to tell their stories to somebody who cares. For whatever reason, I think it's easier for them to confide in a complete stranger than to their loved ones about what has happened to them.

Often when I visit these people they have only been out of combat for a few days and are still in a state of shock. Their wounds are fresh and their emotions are raw. Despite my best efforts to cheer these folks up, these appearances often end with tears.

Although I have gone in alone, it's usually best to share the hospital experience with another comedian so you can have somebody to work off of when things get awkward. My first time, I learned from one of the best, Colin Quinn. The gravelly-voiced Brooklynite is a specialist at cheering up sick people. Colin knelt before each marine's bed, looked them in the eyes very seriously, and said: "Two gay guys are sitting around their apartment. The first gay guy says, 'I'm bored, let's play hide-and-seek. If you find me, you can fuck me.' The other guy says, 'What if I don't find you?' The first gay guy says, 'I'll be behind the couch.' "

Colin's joke always got a big laugh, but I soon learned that in some situations, jokes only go so far. Since then, I've been accompanied on these hospital visits by a variety of entertainers, including Joey Pantoliano, whom most of the patients immediately recognized as the psychopath who savagely beat a stripper to death on *The Sopranos*. I thought, who better to cheer up a victim of horrific violence than a guy who was beheaded on pay cable?

One time I was even teamed up with a cute quartet of Dallas Cowboy Cheerleaders. An ordinary man would be thrilled, but as a Roastmaster, this made me nervous. Would they get my jokes? Would they be offended? Would they upstage me? Would they find out I had a girlfriend? I was up half the night stressing about it. I wanted to do a good job.

The next morning on the way over to the hospital, I talked Nicole, Megan, Sarah, and Christina into letting me enter the soldiers' rooms just ahead of them. I figured that way I could get a few laughs before everyone got distracted by four gorgeous cheerleaders with matching camel toes.

As I entered the first room, I was surprised to find not the guy injured by a roadside bomb that I was expecting but a tired-looking older couple watching *The Price Is Right*. I said, "Hello, my name is Jeff Ross—I'm a comedian from the USO and I came by to say hi to Jeremy. Is he around?" They pointed to the bed. That's when I noticed the outline of a person curled up in the corner under a pile of blankets.

"Um . . . Hey, Jeremy. How you doing, man?" I said to the blankets. Jeremy grunted from underneath. His parents just shrugged. I was afraid to push him too hard because I knew Bethesda Naval Hospital specializes in head injuries and I had already seen a number of these guys during my previous visit. Ever so gently I tried again. "Hey . . . um . . . Jeremy, trust me, I guarantee I'm the goofiest-lookin' person in the room. People say my nose looks like an elbow." Another grunt. "Rarely do you see a face like mine without a tennis ball in its mouth." Crickets. So I jumped to the finale. "Well, anyway, Jeremy, before I go I just wanted you to meet some friends of mine . . . please welcome the Dallas Cowboy Cheerleaders!"

Still nothing! He must've thought I was putting him on. Then I waved the girls in. When he heard them jiggle through the doorway, Jeremy finally peeked out from under his blankets. I could see that he was a good-looking guy with no visible scars. Nicole squealed with a Texas twang, "Hey, handsome! Come on out from under your tent, ya big stud!" That's all it took. Suddenly the blankets were off and the cheerleaders were all sitting on his bed posing for pictures and talking football. His parents beamed at him happily. I never did find out what his injury was, but clearly his libido was in better shape than his sense of humor.

Still, I was glad I had made an attempt. Sometimes being a Roastmaster can be daunting. But, whether your material goes over or not, it's important for a Roastmaster to at least try to inject laughs wherever people need them the most.

The renowned Roastmaster Bob Hope used to get teased by his peers over how many benefits he performed at every year, but he wore that reputation as a badge of honor. He must've known what I'm still learning—that there's no better feeling than picking someone up when they're feeling really low. As Bob Hope used to say, "Have jokes, will travel."

ADDING INSULT TO INJURY

During a recent visit to Walter Reed Army Medical Center I met a soldier named Brendan Marrocco who lost all of his arms and legs in an explosion. One of his eyes is also badly damaged. He joked about winning "the shit lottery." When his optometrist came in to examine him Brendan teased, "No rush, Doc, I'm still blind in that eye!" When his girlfriend held up three fingers he kidded her that he saw six. Then I flipped him the bird and said, "How many am I holding up?" We both laughed. But then his dad briefly lamented his son's loss of vision. I told Brendan he'd already seen the world. Brendan told me he'd really only seen Afghanistan and Staten Island. I told him his funny bone was still intact. He nodded toward the bigger of his two bandaged stumps and said, "Just this one." Then we bumped elbows and Brendan left for a physical therapy session and I went home.

It's people like Brendan who help me keep my own life in perspective. How can I bother sweating the small stuff when soldiers like him are taking on such immense challenges with spirit and a sense of humor?

Occasionally skeptical friends ask me why I'm willing to drop everything and go to Godforsaken places like hospitals and war zones to tell jokes. The answer is because it's the least I can do for people who sacrifice so much. Plus I can't resist a great audience. In fact, it wasn't until I began visiting our troops that I fully understood the job description of being a comedian and the responsibilities of being an American.

MY TIPS FOR TOASTING FRIENDS AND FAMILY

I AM OFTEN ASKED TO MAKE a funny speech at family functions. This is much more nerve-racking than performing for strangers. If I offend, I could lose more than a fan. I could lose an inheritance. In fact, it's been years and my aunt Bess still hasn't forgiven me for calling her "Aunt-Arctica" after she almost knocked the gravy boat over with her arm fat while reaching for a third helping of mashed potatoes one Thanksgiving.

Still, I feel an obligation to accept invitations to honor my friends on special occasions such as weddings, bachelor parties, and sometimes even funerals. When comic legend Jan Murray passed away, I looked out at the packed chapel and said, "Look at this turnout for Jan . . . nothing but old people and their parents!" If an occasion is tense, sad, or stuffy, a little humor can really lighten the mood.

Friends often call me for advice before making a toast at a party. I usually tell them to have fun, talk slowly, keep it short, and speak from the heart. I also recommend going on right after dessert is served. By then the crowd has a few drinks in 'em and has been fully fed. Nothing is funny when you're hungry.

Below I offer five tips for making toasts. I call them the five F's . . .

1. FRIENDLY

Keep it friendly. Always try to shmooze before you slam. Remember, you want your friends to still like you afterward. Example: "Hey, Roger, you're the best roommate I ever had, but your breath smells like an anchovy's cunt." This is a potentially offensive joke, but because it is delivered in the form of a backhanded compliment about being a great roommate, you're off the hook.

2. FAST

Timing is everything. Comedic opportunities often come and go in a flash, so stay alert. For example, if an old man wanders into the room late and looking lost, it almost doesn't matter what you say as long as you get it out instantaneously. "What's the matter, gramps? Lose your golf ball?" Stay in the moment. Insult humor is a reflex.

3. FUNNY

A joke is either funny or not funny. Don't try to analyze why. Follow your gut instincts. And remember, if a joke doesn't offend somebody somewhere, it's not funny. Right now there's a kid in Utah whose pet chicken just got hit by a car while crossing the road. Fuck him too.

4. FUCK

After years of on-the-job research, I have concluded that tossing in the word "fuck" gives even the most rudimentary insult or joke some added oomph. Examples: "Nice tie, fuckface!" "Uncle Joe, is that a new suit or did you fuck the drapes?" "Hey, Grandma, go fuck yourself."

5. FOND FAREWELL

After you've called somebody every name in this book, it's usually a good idea to shake hands and say something nice at the end. Hugs work, too. On occasion I have also sent flowers and hand-written notes. It is also useful to keep substantial amounts of cash around just in case something goes completely haywire.

I'll never forget the time Buddy Hackett was making a speech at our friend Barry Katz's wedding when suddenly a strange hum began emanating from the electric keyboard set up beside him. Buddy was a master speechmaker, but this noise was gradually becoming more and more of a distraction to him. Plus, Buddy battled with performance anxiety in his later years and was only making this toast because the best man had dragged him up there.

Before long, the hum escalated to a buzz and Buddy started getting really peeved. As he reached the end of his toast, instead of lifting his full glass of champagne in the air in honor of the bride and groom, he simply poured the whole thing into the keyboard. With alcohol now seeping through the wiring, the electric piano began emitting a noise akin to what I imagine a dolphin sounds like when it's getting banged by a great white whale.

Suddenly a curtain opened up behind Buddy and four guys

dressed as the Beatles during the *Sgt. Pepper's Lonely Hearts Club Band* era came running out with panicked looks on their powdered faces. Their precious vintage keyboard was ruined. Buddy started cursing and the bride, Susanna Brisk, a comedian in her own right who can usually take a hit, looked like she was about to stab Buddy with the cake knife. Her family members, most of whom had flown in from Russia and Australia for the occasion, began murmuring in disgust and confusion.

As Buddy headed for the exit, I intercepted him to see if he was okay. Matter-of-factly he said, "Please tell Barry and Susanna I'm sorry. I gotta go." A short time later a messenger showed up with two thick envelopes: one for the bride and groom; one for the band.

My point is: No matter how much it fucking costs, a Roastmaster needs fucking silence while he's fucking speaking. As the Beatles used to sing, "Money can't buy you love"—but it sure can get you out of a pickle.

A ROASTMASTER
NEEDS A MENTOR

I MENTION BUDDY HACKETT MANY TIMES in this book. Not only was he one of the greatest Roastmasters of all time, he was my best friend and the smartest guy I knew. In fact, comedy was about twentieth on the list of his areas of expertise. For hours, we'd sit in large swinging rope chairs in his cactus-filled backyard and chat about everything from politics to pizza, poker to pussy, and premises to punch lines. But since this book is about roasting we'll stay on topic.

Whenever I had a big roast coming up, I would always run my material by Buddy first. He was an expert in talking dirty, knew right where the line was, and never let me cross it. If a joke might seem like it could be particularly insensitive, Buddy would usually advise me not to do it. "Don't hurt anybody," he would say. His rationale was that even though a super-edgy joke may get the biggest laugh of the night and may even get quoted in the newspapers the next day, it's still not worth it, because even if that person laughs along, they might actually be offended. He further

reasoned that most people will never bother to tell you they're upset, instead you'll just quietly lose them as a friend.

Buddy didn't have this problem. Everybody loved him. Especially me. I still wear his black onyx cuff links or one of the silk bow ties and cravats Buddy used to wear onstage on special roasting occasions. When he first presented them as a gift after his retirement, I remember his warning me not to wear them with too tight a collar because if I felt restricted it would negatively affect my overall performance.

Over the years Buddy dropped many other useful Hackett-isms on me, such as "Never listen to advice from someone who hasn't walked the last thirty feet." In other words, don't pay too much attention to people who watch from the wings. Buddy's rationale was that only other performers truly understand what it's like to be alone onstage in front of an audience, armed with only a microphone.

As a kid, I recall my parents laughing at the risqué stories and witty one-liners Buddy told Johnny Carson long after my bedtime. I used to hide quietly at the top of the stairs and listen to my parents laugh hysterically, as his cartoonish voice bellowed out the side of his mouth and through our TV. Sometimes I even smelled some weird smoke coming from downstairs, but that's another story.

The first time I actually saw Buddy perform live was at a casino in Atlantic City. I was a new comedian working a comedy club in town and stayed an extra day to catch Buddy's show at the Trump. I remember his funny son Sandy Hackett doing about twenty minutes of jokes about his dad before introducing him. I also recall sitting there all alone thinking how incredibly cool it was that father and son got to go on tour together.

Within sixty seconds of being introduced, Buddy called a woman in the front row a "cunt" because she was taking notes. He said he didn't approve of note-taking during his act. She said that she was a reporter for a local newspaper. He told her to fuck off and die. It was an uncomfortable moment for the audience, but it didn't seem to matter. Within seconds Buddy had every man, woman, and waiter rolling in the aisles with involved stories filled with short jokes, such as, "My wife said to me, 'I want to be cremated.' I said, 'How about Tuesday?'"

Then for another hour Buddy roasted the entire front section before finishing up with a ten-minute routine about driving with no pants on in the middle of the night to get his pregnant wife a pizza pie. As the audience gave him a standing ovation, Buddy returned to the mic and said, "You treat every performer the way you treated me, you'll never see a bad show!" Then he turned on his heels and danced triumphantly off the stage.

Years later, when I got to know him, I asked him why he might've called that woman a cunt at the very top of his performance. Buddy said he often walked out onstage and dug himself a hole just to see how long it took him to get out of it. "That's how I keep it interesting," he confessed.

Buddy also told me back then he required that his employers keep the showroom at a crisp sixty degrees in order to keep the crowd awake and lively. "Nothing drains the audience's energy like sweating," he said. That's right, Roastmasters, if you want the crowd alert, keep their nipples pert. Buddy also told me that he gave this advice to David Letterman as he was preparing to launch his original late-night program.

Buddy loved to pass the wisdom of his experiences on to young comedians. After all, he'd made countless TV appearances;

acted in more than twenty movies, including *The Music Man, The Little Mermaid*, and *It's a Mad Mad Mad Mad World*; he sang and danced in some great Broadway musicals; hammed it up in dozens of commercials; and ripped the roof off countless nightclubs before finally retiring in his seventies, due to, believe it or not, "stage fright." By then his performing was limited to yearly benefits in support of stray animals and daily phone calls to friends. In fact, nearly every morning Buddy would think of a new joke and call the first five people who popped into his head. Usually something short and sweet like, "Last night at the ball game I was so drunk I took a hot dog into the men's room and tried to teach it to piss." If I was asleep Buddy would talk into my answering machine until I woke up to hear his new joke. I grew to love his morning wake-up calls. Buddy's voice was my comedy caffeine.

It was during these later years in his life that we really got to know each other. In fact, we talked almost every day ("Hiya, Buddy!" "Hiya, pal!") and he even wrote a letter of personal reference on my behalf to a co-op board, in which he described me as "almost like one of my children." On Sunday mornings (which is noon for comedians), Buddy would invite me over and cook me breakfast. Although I was practically raised in a catering hall, he would never let me touch anything. As he fried up some savory matzoh brei with salami and onions, Buddy told me stories about his days as an upholsterer in Brooklyn, a soldier in World War II, and a "tummler" on the Borscht Belt circuit. His eyes would inevitably well up with tears as his mind raced back to his earlier self, the young Leonard Hacker, who toiled every summer either as a bellhop or a waiter at the famed Catskill Mountain hotels in upstate New York.

As his natural talent and lovability became evident, the Concord Hotel promoted him to tummler, which is basically a roving comedian who walks around the pool area cracking jokes for the guests. In fact, this is how he met his wife, Sherry, who was a dance instructor at the same hotel. Eventually they got married and he became Buddy Hackett, a Catskills comedian trying to make it big.

Then one day a man named Jules White called and offered to triple his income. Over the phone from Hollywood, the famed producer and director of the Three Stooges films explained to Buddy that Curly Howard had suffered a stroke. They wanted Buddy to move out west immediately and join the Three Stooges as his replacement. Buddy told me how he agonized over what to do. After all, he now had a wife and young son to support, with another kid on the way. In the end, Buddy bet on himself and turned down the chance to be part of a comedy team. "I just didn't want to wake up every morning and wonder how the other two guys were feeling," Buddy explained, as I swallowed a bite of mouthwatering matzoh brei. In the kitchen, as onstage, Buddy was a solo artist.

Of course, it's not uncommon for comedians to get offered tempting sums to take gigs that don't feel quite right. One time I was offered big bucks for hosting a weeklong "Let's Make a Deal-a-Thon" on the Game Show Network. That night on the phone I lamented to Buddy that it would be great to have that fat paycheck, but that I'd feel like a sell-out for hosting such a cheesy show. "I'd rather be respected than rich," I said. He shot back, "Fuck the respect—take the money. Nobody will ever see that piece of shit show." In the end, Buddy was right. The show came and went and I used that money to produce a documentary about my first trip to Iraq to entertain the troops.

Sure, Buddy was my mentor, but we were more like brothers than anything else. The only time he ever got mad at me was the day he was to get a distinguished New Yorker award from Mayor Rudolph Giuliani. Buddy had flown in from Los Angeles especially for the occasion and I agreed to ride with him in his limo to the early morning event at City Hall.

Buddy emerged from his apartment on Roosevelt Island in a crisp beige suit with a colorful tie, looking more dapper than I'd ever seen him. As he got into the limo he immediately began leering incredulously at the filled-to-the-brim grande latte from Starbucks that I was balancing on my lap. Just as we pulled out we hit a small bump in the street and a tiny drop of coffee flew out of my cup and landed about a millimeter from Buddy's trousers. It was only a close call, but Buddy still blew up at me like I'd just tried to murder one of his cats. (Did I mention he kept twenty-two cats in his backyard?) Buddy then made the limo driver pull over so I could dump my expensive latte into the gutter. We eventually got to City Hall, where the mayor called the former Leonard Hacker from Brooklyn "one of the funniest men in the world," before spilling half a can of Dr Pepper all over his sleeve.

In his six-decades-long career, Buddy worked with everybody from Frank Sinatra to Carol Burnett. He had seen all the great modern-day stand-up comedians come and go. One day as we hung out on the rope chairs, feeding the cats, I asked him who he thought was the funniest person of his time. Buddy said, "Everybody great is considered the funniest for a while." He went on to explain to me that nearly every respected comedian has a moment when they either tell a certain joke or appear in such a memorable role that it causes the entire country to take notice. I took great relief in hearing this information. It was so nice to know that if I was willing to be patient and work until I'm a hundred years old, I will eventually have my moment on top.

One of the most technical pieces of comedy wisdom Buddy ever offered me was about "peeling the onion." He explained that every joke premise has an infinite amount of possibilities. "If you're willing to unravel all the angles and peel back the layers," he said, "a routine could go on indefinitely." Buddy was famous for telling winding stories onstage full of hilarious imagery and imaginative callbacks. Watching him motivated me to take a one-liner about my hundred-and-four-year-old aunt-tique and turn it into an epic monologue about how she was trampled at a Wu Tang concert. Thanks to Buddy's influence, that bit is now so memorable fans request it at my shows.

However, one piece of Buddy's advice I did not take was, "Never ever get involved in the politics of the Friars Club." Buddy's reasoning was that the club was a place for comics to unwind and have fun. But when I was nominated to be the youngest member of the board of governors, I couldn't resist running for office.

In the end, Buddy was right—again. It was a nightmare constantly arguing with the old guard about things like the price of a brisket sandwich in the dining room and whom we should roast next. Still, being on the board did enable me to convince the Friars Club to finally allow their private roasts to be televised. Sometimes a Roastmaster must shake things up.

Still, I continue to think about my best pal every day. Not just because I miss him so much, but because with every new decision life brings I find myself wondering, "What would Buddy say?"

A ROASTMASTER MUST MAINTAIN A SHITTY ATTITUDE

*W*ARNING: MOST PEOPLE THINK IT'S a breeze being a Roastmaster. Even my fans think I sniff half a bottle of glue, chase a martini with a double scotch, and then prance up to the podium and wing it. (I can assure you this was true only at the Pam Anderson roast—everybody was doing it.)

The truth is that being a successful insult comic is a perilous mental tightrope requiring constant concentration and unswerving diligence. When I walk into a room, I need to size up at least eight things to insult within four seconds or I feel completely naked. If I'm the only one in the room I may just have to roast the drapes or the silverware. "Fuck you, spoon—you're nothing but a gay fork."

However, the most precarious thing about being a high-stakes, big-time, nationally televised, internationally lauded fuck-you artist is maintaining a horrible attitude even when life is very good. Happiness can seriously interfere with one's ability to deride, belittle, and sneer at things. It is imperative for a professional purveyor of put-downs to stay in touch with the essential futility and misery of life.

There are many ways of doing this. I've heard that Don Rickles reads a lot of French existentialist philosophy. During his vaudeville days, Fat Jack E. Leonard would pay a hobo to kick him in the balls every morning. If you happen to be ugly, it might help to look in the mirror a lot. If you're not ugly, find someone who is and stare at them for a while. If they're ugly, they certainly won't mind the attention.

For a true Roastmaster, life itself is a roast. Don't let any yaysayers infect your thinking with positive energy, and be sure to surround yourself with people who annoy you. It'll all be worth it when you finally get to the end of your first roast—the part when you say something nice. After immersing yourself in shittiness, this moment of sunshine will feel genuinely illuminating—especially if you've been drinking.

I must also warn you that, like skydiving or bull riding, high-level dissing can be exhilarating but also very hazardous to your health. My fellow Friar Bob Greenberg had an uncle, who had an uncle who was a vaudeville comedian named Al Kelly, who specialized in double-talk. One day he was killing at a Friars roast when suddenly, on his very last punch line, he had a stroke and collapsed right there on the podium. Everybody thought it was part of the act. By the time the laughs died down, a doctor in the house pronounced him dead. Not only was it sad that he passed away so suddenly, but it was also very hard for the next act to follow.

Then of course there was the time yours truly was roasting showbiz icon Jerry Lewis. Although I was asked by the producers not to make any jokes about Jerry's charity work on behalf of kids with muscular dystrophy, I couldn't help taking it right to the line. I said, "We've all been making fun of Jerry Lewis today, but I say, what about the good things that Jerry Lewis does? What about the fact that just this past Labor Day, a six-year-old kid got up out of his wheelchair and walked for the first time . . . to turn off the Jerry Lewis Telethon." Jerry laughed so hard I seriously thought he was going to have a heart attack. He didn't. But he did

ME ATTEMPTING TO MURDER JERRY LEWIS IN FRONT OF ROBERT DENIRO AND MARTIN SCORSESE.

have one during his flight home the next morning. Luckily, he got to a hospital quickly and was okay. My point is: Be careful and keep a respirator on hand at all times. Also, don't roast anybody over eighty-two. It's just too risky.

At some point you may have wondered why I have chosen to give away so many of my secrets. It's because I don't see roasting as a competitive sport. I see it as a fraternal endeavor. I love roasting, I love roasters, and I love you just for getting to the end of *I Only Roast the Ones I Love*. There is nothing I would like more than for a young wise guy or wise gal to study my teachings and learn from my experiences in order to become America's next great roaster. Without the infusion of new blood and new ideas, the art of the roast will surely die. So perhaps it is up to you, my potentially funny friend, to continue the traditions set forth in this book.

At the time of this writing the economy is in shambles. The banking, airline, automotive, and newspaper industries are laying people off by the score. This means we'll start to see a whole new generation of lost souls leave the corporate ranks to join our ranks as American Roastmasters—that is, if prostitution and three-card monte prove unsuccessful. Right now our country needs rookie Roastmasters more than usual. The demand for the services we provide, mainly comic relief and brutal honesty, is currently spiking higher than Woody Harrelson jamming with Snoop Dogg at a Dave Matthews Band concert.

But whether you decide to roast as a hobby or as a career, I implore you to keep three basic principles in mind. . . . Number one: Have fun. Number two: Enjoy the process. Number three: Never apologize. A Roastmaster must take ownership of what he says.

Now you too have the knowledge. The entire world is your dais. Go forth and carry a big shtick!

Until then, stop moving your lips while you read. You look like an idiot.

Respectfully,
Jeffrey Ross, Roastmaster General
of the United States of America

ROASTKNOWLEDGMENTS

Writing a book is a lonely ordeal filled with long nights and tons of Chinese food. Still, I couldn't have done it without the help of supportive friends at Simon Spotlight Entertainment, The William Morris Endeavor Agency, New Wave Entertainment, Six Point Harness Studio, Comedy Central, The New York Friars Club, and my pharmacist Elliot Winestock.

I also want to express my gratitude to the following individuals . . .

Broadcast legend Howard Stern, who first suggested I write a book about roasting.

My eternally enthusiastic pal Brian Stern, who took Howard's suggestion seriously enough to find me a book agent.

My sophisticated and skilled book agents Erin Malone and Tracy Fisher, who wrote the proposal and created this opportunity for an underground comedian to write a big-time book.

The powerful visionary Jen Bergstrom, who stepped right up and made me an offer to be an author.

My brilliant and beautiful editor Trish Boczkowski, who expertly guided me through an otherwise terrifying process—and occasionally saved me from sounding like a complete schmuck. Seriously, she's really fucking smart. If any of you ever write a book you should beg her to edit it.

Trish's overqualified and overworked assistant Cara Bedick, who kept us on track through countless revisions, long weekends, and nervous breakdowns.

A comedy scholar named Abe Hurwicz, who offered up his wit and wisdom to every aspect of this project. Somebody please give him a bath and a book deal!

My positive-vibes-providing manager Barry Katz, who read every chapter as soon as it was written and immediately responded with, "AWESOME," even when the material wasn't yet up to snuff.

The imaginative pairing of Michael Nagin and Justin Borucki, who designed and photographed a killer cover. Still, I would have gone with a topless picture of Bea Arthur.

The funny and daring Sah Tantivaranyoo, whose mind-blowing illustrations made the book feel complete. His work should be in a stoner museum.

My personal lawyers Todd Rubenstein, David Krintzman, and Jared Levine for making sure I don't get ripped off, locked up, or kicked out.

Simon Spotlight's diligent and delightful Elisa Rivlin, for making sure I didn't include anything in this book that could get me killed, or worse, sued.

My trusted consiglieres Harvey Altman, Deborah Gale, and Dan Adler for making sure I don't blow my advance on chocolate chip cheesecake and Springsteen tickets.

The thorough and tenacious Jen Robinson, who sought out

every angle publicizing this book—thus making me the first author interviewed for the magazines *Every Day with Rachael Ray* and *Penthouse* in the same morning.

My girlfriend Megan, who lay in bed patiently reading my prose aloud while I obsessed over my puns instead of her panties.

My extremely supportive sister, Robyn, who had the balls to tell me when something wasn't funny.

Must give it up to my homeys who helped or encouraged me during the process . . . Kii Arens, Brendan Burch, Eddy Friedfeld, Doug Miller, Eric "Dosage" Fingerhut, Andrew Jarecki, Bob Saget, Eric Stahl, Jimmy Kimmel, Ralphie May, Stacy Mark, "The Robe," Ray James, Matt Harowitz, James Smith, Amy Zvi, Justin Silvera, Jeff Kravitz, Bill Zehme, Mike Ferruchi, Chris Maguire, Steve Ross, Debbie Keller, Heidi Feign, Jay Karas, Erwin Moore, Aaron Lee, Mike Rowe, Cousin Kenny, and my cousin Aron.

To all the proofreaders at Simon Spotlight who diligently worked on this manuscript I say . . . Thank yoU!

I'd also like to give a shout out to my fellow Friars—especially our Dean Freddie Roman, our Abbot Jerry Lewis, our Executive Director Michael Gyrue, and our roast producer Mark Krantz.

Not to mention the dedicated Friars family including Michael Caputo, Barry Dougherty, Stewie Stone, Stu Cantor, Alison Grambs, Larry Gerard, Giuseppe Tarillo, Cynthia Brown, Liz Nieves, Lydia the receptionist, and a bunch of rather unattractive waiters for their incredible support and sarcasm all these years.

Special props to my Friars fathers Jean-Pierre Trebot and Gianfranco "Frank here!" Capitelli, for believing in me from the beginning.

Also, hats off to the legendary Doug Herzog for having the vision to see how big the roasts could be.

And lastly, a big salute to an innovative executive named Elizabeth Porter and a dictatorial director named Joel Gallen, who continually invite me to say whatever the hell I want on TV. Without them this book would have been a pamphlet.

Thanks, everybody! I love you all! Yashar Koach! (Your strength should be straight.)

ART CREDITS